Bertolt B

The Good Soul of Szechuan

translated by
David Harrower

Methuen Drama

Published by Methuen Drama, 2008

1 3 5 7 9 10 8 6 4 2

Methuen Drama
A & C Black Publishers Limited
38 Soho Square
London W1D 3HB
www.acblack.com

Translation copyright for the play © 1985 by Stefan S. Brecht

David Harrower has asserted his right to be identified as the translator of this work

Original work entitled *Der gute Mensch von Sezuan*
Copyright © 1955 by Suhrkamp Verlag, Berlin

All rights reserved

ISBN: 978 1 408 10965 6

A CIP catalogue record for this book is available from the British Library.

Typeset by Country Setting, Kingsdown, Kent
Printed and bound in Great Britain by
Cox & Wyman Ltd, Reading Berkshire

Caution

The Good Soul
of Szechuan

by Bertolt Brecht
translation by David Harrower

This production opened at the Young Vic on 8 May 2008

THE GOOD SOUL OF SZECHUAN

by Bertolt Brecht

translation by David Harrower

God 3 **Steven Beard**
Mrs Shin/Movement Direction **Linda Dobell**
Policeman/Priest **Gareth Farr**
Wang **Adam Gillen**
Carpenter/Mr Shu Fu **Shiv Grewal**
Shen Te/Shui Ta **Jane Horrocks**
Yang Sun **John Marquez**
Agent/Trumpet **Sam O'Mahony-Adams**
Nephew/Piano/Musical Direction **David Osmond**
God 1 **Susan Porrett**
Wife **Sophie Russell**
Mrs Mitzu/Mrs Yang **Liza Sadovy**
Father **Tom Silburn**
God 2 **Michelle Wade**

Direction **Richard Jones**
Design **Miriam Buether**
Costume **Nicky Gillibrand**
Light **Paule Constable**
Music and Sound **David Sawer**
Associate Sound Design **Sarah Weltman**
Casting **Julia Horan CDG**
Assistant Direction **Anna Dirckinck-Holmfeld**
Assistant Design **Olan Wrynn**

Wigs **Campbell Young**
Costume Supervisor **Claire Murphy**
Assistant Costume Supervisor **Bryony Fayers**
Costume Makers **Keith Watson & Pauline Parker**
Wardrobe Assistants/Dressers **Geri Spencer & Anu Bankole**
Wardrobe Work Placements **Hannah Chilton & Penny Scuthorpe**

Stage Manager **Julia Reid**
Deputy Stage Manager **Jenny Grand**
Assistant Stage Manager **Rebecca Ridley**
Props Buyers **Anthony Newman & Sun Ling**

Literal Translation **Laura Gribble**

Scenery built in the Young Vic workshops by **Paul Halter, Chris Shepherd, Gibson Arpino, Nathan Davidson** (work experience) and by **Factory Settings**

Stage Crew **Ben Porter**

With thanks to **Toyota Material Handling UK, Keith King at A.P.S. Plant Services LTD, David Pearce at W Pearce LTD**

Bertolt Brecht Playwright

Bertolt Brecht was born in Augsburg on 10 February 1898 and died in Berlin on 14 August 1956. He grew to maturity as a playwright in the frenetic years of the twenties and early thirties, with such plays as *Man Equals Man, The Threepenny Opera* and *The Mother*. He left Germany when Hitler came to power in 1933, eventually reaching the United States in 1941, where he remained until 1947. It was during this period of exile that such masterpieces as *Life of Galileo, Mother Courage and Her Children* and *The Caucasian Chalk Circle* were written. Shortly after his return to Europe in 1947 he founded the Berliner Ensemble, and from then until his death was mainly occupied in producing his own plays.

The Good Soul of Szechuan was written between 1939 and 1941 and completed in 1943.

David Harrower Translation

Previous adaptations include: Pirandello's *Six Characters in Search of an Author* (Young Vic); Chekhov's *Ivanov* (National Theatre); Buchner's *Woyzeck* (Lyceum Theatre Edinburgh); Jon Fosse's *The Girl on the Sofa* (Edinburgh International Festival and the Schaubuhne, Berlin); Horvarth's *Tales from the Vienna Woods* (National Theatre); and Schiller's *Mary Stuart* (National Theatre of Scotland).

Original works include: *Knives in Hens* (Traverse Theatre); *54% Acrylic* (for BBC Radio 4); *Kill the Old Torture Their Young* (Traverse Theatre); *Presence* (Royal Court); *Dark Earth* (Traverse); *Blackbird* (Edinburgh International Festival).

BIOGRAPHIES

Steven Beard God 3

Theatre and opera includes: *Racing Demon, Le Bourgeois Gentilhomme, A Midsummer Night's Dream* (National Theatre); *Endgame* (Nottingham Playhouse and Weimar); *A Flea in Her Ear, The Illusion* (Old Vic); *La Bête* (Lyric Hammersmith); *Seven Doors, Nathan the Wise, Scapino* (Chichester Festival Theatre); *Of Thee I Sing, Paradise Moscow* (Opera North); *Much Ado About Nothing, King John* (RSC).
Film includes: *Shakespeare in Love.*

Linda Dobell

Mrs Shin / Movement Direction
Theatre and opera includes: *Asylum* (Nigel Charnock Co.); *Holy Mothers* (Ambassador's Theatre); *The Pleasure Man* (Citizen's Theatre, Glasgow); *The Miser* (National Theatre); *The Lower Depths* (Cardboard Citizens); *Crock of Gold* (London Bubble Theatre); *Lady Macbeth of Mtsensk* (Royal Opera House); *A Midsummer Night's Dream* (RSC); *Lulu, From Morning to Midnight* (ENO); *The Queen of Spades, Hansel and Gretel* (WNO); *Macbeth* (Glyndebourne).

Gareth Farr Policeman / Priest

Theatre includes: *Hobson's Choice* (Young Vic); *In Celebration* (Duke of York's); *How Many Miles to Basra* (West Yorkshire Playhouse); *The Long, the Short and the Tall* (Sheffield Crucible); *Harvest* (Royal Court); *A Midsummer Night's Dream* (RSC); *Brassed Off* (York Theatre Royal); *The Taming of the Shrew* (Salisbury Playhouse).

Television includes: *Holby City, Doctors, Britz, The Bill, Turkish Delight, Jonathan Creek, Heartbeat.*

Adam Gillen Wang

Theatre includes: *The Lion's Mouth* (Royal Court Rough Cuts); *The Five Wives of Maurice Pinder* (National Theatre).
Television includes: *Oliver Twist.*
Film includes: *Hippie Hippie Shake.*

Shiv Grewal Carpenter / Mr Shu Fu

Shiv was a member of the Radio Drama Company.
Theatre includes: *Too Close to Home* (Manchester Library); *Rafta Rafta* (National Theatre); *Gladiator Games* (Sheffield Crucible); *A Fine Balance* (Hampstead Theatre); *Twelfth Night* (Albery Theatre); *Strictly Dandia* (Edinburgh Festival); *Balti Kings* (West Yorkshire Playhouse); *A Midsummer Night's Dream* (London Bubble Theatre); *A Streetcar Named Desire* (Sherman Theatre, Cardiff).
Television and radio includes: *Messiah III, Second Generation, The Archers, Book at Bedtime.*
Film includes: *Brothers in Trouble, Felicia's Journey.*

Jane Horrocks Shen Te / Shui Ta

Theatre includes: *The Rise and Fall of Little Voice* (National Theatre and Aldwych); *Cabaret* (Donmar); *Absurd Person Singular* (Garrick).
Television includes: *Road, Bad Girl, Absolutely Fabulous, Suffer the Little Children, Never Mind the Horrocks, The Street.*
Film includes: *The Dressmaker, The Witches, Life Is Sweet, Little Voice, Chicken Run, Corpse Bride.*

John Marquez Yang Sun
Theatre includes: *Streetcar to Tennessee* (Young Vic); *The Hypochondriac, The Chain Play* (Almeida); *The Emperor Jones, Market Boy, Sing Your Heart Out for the Lads, Baby Doll* (National Theatre); *Local, Mother Theresa is Dead, Twins* (Royal Court).
Television includes: *Gunrush, Doc Martin, Hotel Babylon, Ronni Ancona & Co.*

Sam O'Mahony-Adams
Agent / Trumpet
Theatre includes: *Mongeo* (Belgrade Theatre, Coventry); *The Taming of the Shrew* (Wilton's Music Hall); *Much Ado About Nothing, King John, Romeo and Juliet* (RSC); *The Beach* (Theatre 503).
Television includes: *Casualty.*

David Osmond
Nephew / Piano / Musical Direction
Theatre includes: *The History Boys* (National Theatre tour and West End); *The Winter's Tale, The Grapes of Wrath, SATB* (Rose Bruford College).

Susan Porrett God 1
Theatre includes: *The London Cuckolds* (Royal Court); *A Month in the Country, Much Ado About Nothing* (National Theatre); *The Art of Success, Macbeth* (RSC); *David Copperfield* (Greenwich Theatre); *Forty Years On* (West Yorkshire Playhouse); *Romeo and Juliet* (English Touring Theatre); *Hay Fever* (Oxford Stage Company).
Television includes: *Upstairs/ Downstairs, Grange Hill, Absolute Hell, Foyle's War, After Thomas.*
Film includes: *A Private Function.*

Sophie Russell Wife
Theatre includes: *The Chaingang Gang, Meat and Two Veg, The Ratcatcher of Hamelin* (Cartoon de Salvo); *The Crock of Gold, Metamorphoses, The Tinderbox, Alice Through the Looking Glass* (London Bubble); *Great Expectations* (Shifting Sands Theatre Co.); *The Bitches' Ball* (Penny Dreadful Theatre Co.); *I am Dandy* (David Gale Ensemble); *Oliver Twist* (TNT Music Theatre); *Cinderella* (Palace, Westcliff); *East Anglian Psychos* (Eastern Angles Theatre Co.); *A Christmas Carol* (Manoel Theatre, Malta).
Television includes: *Wire in the Blood.*

Liza Sadovy Mrs Mitzu / Mrs Yang
Theatre and opera includes:
Six Characters Looking for an Author (Young Vic); *Sunday in the Park with George* (Menier Chocolate Factory and Wyndham's); *The Dresser* (Peter Hall Company at the Duke of York's); *Tales from the Vienna Woods, The Heiress* (National Theatre); *Alice in Wonderland* (RSC); *Company* (Donmar and Albery); *The Marriage of Figaro* (Music Theatre London); *Into the Woods* (Phoenix and West End).
Television and radio includes: *Extras, Midsomer Murders, Prime Suspect, The Archers.*
Film includes: *Topsy Turvey; Sweeney Todd.*

Tom Silburn Father
Theatre includes: *Two Princes*
(Clwyd Theatr Cymru); *Chasing the
Moment* (Arcola); *Dr. Faustus*
(Bristol Old Vic); *On the Third Day*
(New Ambassadors); *5/11,
The Government Inspector, King Lear,
The Master and Margarita,
A Midsummer Night's Dream*
(Chichester Festival Theatre); *Of Mice
and Men* (Birmingham Rep).
Film includes: *King Lear, The Trench.*
Radio includes: *James Baldwin in
Paris, Killing Mr Mort, States of Mind.*

Michelle Wade God 2
Theatre and opera includes:
Six Characters Looking for an Author
(Young Vic); *The Wild Duck*
(Lyric Hammersmith); *Man and
Superman* (West End);
*Romeo and Juliet, Othello,
The Importance of Being Earnest*
(Leeds Playhouse);
My Mother Said I Never Should
(Contact Theatre, Manchester);
The Seagull, The Glass Menagerie
(Manchester); *The Wind in the Willows*
(Royal Opera House);
A Midsummer Night's Dream (RSC).

Richard Jones Direction
Theatre and opera includes:
*Six Characters Looking For An Author,
Hobson's Choice* (Young Vic); *La Bête*
(Broadway and West End);
Titanic (Broadway);
Billy Budd (Frankfurt); *Lady Macbeth
Of Mtsensk* (Royal Opera House and
La Scala); *Wozzeck* (Komische Berlin
and WNO); *Into The Woods*
(Phoenix Theatre); *Hansel And Gretel*
(WNO and The Met, New York);
The Trojans (ENO); *The Fiery Angel*
(La Monnaie,Brussels); Wagner's
*Ring Cycle, Gianni Schicchi &
L'Heure Espagnole* (Royal Opera
House); *Tales From The Vienna Woods*
(National Theatre); *The Cunning Little
Vixen* (Amsterdam).

Miriam Buether Design
Theatre and opera includes:
generations (Young Vic); *My Child, The
Wonderful World Of Dissocia* (Royal
Court); *The Bacchae, Realism*
(National Theatre of Scotland); *Trade*
(RSC and Soho Theatre);
Sacrifice (WNO); *Death Of Klinghoffer*
(Scottish Opera); *The Bee*
(Soho Theatre and Tokyo);
After The End (Paines Plough);
Long Time Dead (Theatre Royal,
Plymouth); *pool (no water)*
(Frantic Assembly); *Guantanamo*
(Tricycle Theatre).
Dance includes: *Outsight and
Tenderhooks* (Foundation Gulbenkian,
Lisbon); *Body of Poetry* (Komische
Oper, Berlin).

Nicky Gillibrand Costumes
Theatre and opera includes:
Vernon God Little (Young Vic);
The Seagull, Powerbook (National
Theatre); *Jumpers* (National Theatre
and Broadway); *Billy Elliot* (West End
and Australia); *The Tempest* (RSC);
By The Bog Of Cats (Wyndham's);
Camille (Lyric Hammersmith);
Lady Macbeth Of Mtsensk
(Royal Opera House and Italy);
*The Wind in the Willows, Gianni
Schicchi & L'Heure Espagnole*(Royal
Opera House); *Rusalka* (Copenhagen);
The Fiery Angel (La Monnaie,
Brussels); *Wozzeck* (Opera North);
Peter Grimes (ENO).

Paule Constable Light
Theatre and opera includes:
Vernon God Little, generations
(Young Vic); *The Man Who Had All the
Luck, Othello* (Donmar Warehouse);
War Horse,
Women of Troy, Saint Joan
(National Theatre); *Satyagraha*
(ENO); *Saint Matthew Passion*
(Glyndebourne); *Death in Venice*
(Bregenz); *Evita* (Adelphi Theatre);
A Moon for the Misbegotten (Old Vic);
Peter Grimes (Opera North);
The Marriage of Figaro
(Royal Opera House).
Dance includes: *Seven Deadly Sins*
(Royal Ballet).

David Sawer Music and Sound
Works include: *cat's-eye* (Lontano),
Hollywood Extra (Matrix Ensemble),
The Memory of Water (BCMG),
Tiroirs (London Sinfonietta), *Songs of
Love and War, Byrnan Wood,
the greatest happiness principle,*

Piano Concerto (all BBC Proms),
From Morning to Midnight (ENO),
Stramm Gedichte (New London
Chamber Choir), *Rebus* (musikFabrik).
Theatre includes: *Jackets* (Bush);
Food of Love (Almeida), *The Blue Ball*
(National Theatre), *Swansong,
The Long Time Ago Story*
(BBC Radio 3).

Julia Horan CDG Casting
Theatre and opera includes:
Lost Highway (ENO and Young Vic);
Tintin (Young Vic and tour);
Swimming with Sharks (Vaudeville);
*A Chain Play, The Homecoming,
Awake and Sing!, Dying for It*
(Almeida); *Out of the Fog* (Almeida
Projects); *Three Sisters on Hope Street*
(Liverpool Everyman and Playhouse,
Hampstead Theatre);
Absolute Beginners (Lyric
Hammersmith); *pool (no water)*
(Frantic Assembly); *Gaddafi – A Living
Myth* (ENO); *Bad Jazz* (ATC);
Kafka's Dick (Watford).

Anna Dirckinck- Holmfeld
Assistant Director
As assistant director: *Rusalka,
L'incoronazione di Poppea,
Vec Makropulos* (Copenhagen Opera
House); *That Face* (Royal Court);
Stallerhof (Southwark Playhouse).
As director:
365 Days / 365 Plays: W29 (Site-spe-
cific theatre piece, London);
*Postmortem (*King's Head Theatre);
The Pinup (White Bear Theatre);
The Dispute (Edinburgh Festival);
Inferno (L'Océan Productions).

THE YOUNG VIC

We are this country's leading home for younger
theatre artists, especially directors. By presenting
seasons of work by new directors in tandem with some
of the great directors of the world - mingling youth and
experience, ambition and genius - we hope to make the
Young Vic one of the most exciting theatres in the world.

Many people, especially the young, believe that theatre belongs to 'others'
of another class, or another generation. But artists create for everyone.
So we keep our prices low and, through an extensive program of
Teaching, Participation and Research, we make a priority of finding and
creating new audiences. 10% of our tickets are given away each year,
irrespective of box-office pressure.

We believe a theatre should be a place of energy, intelligence and
pleasure.

Join us whenever you can.

Young Vic
66 The Cut
London SE1 8LZ

www.youngvic.org
Tickets & Administration 020 7922 2922
Administration 020 7922 2800

The Young Vic is a company limited by guarantee, registered in England No. 1188209.
VAT registration No. 236 673 348
The Young Vic (registered charity number 268876) receives public funding from:

Supporting the Young Vic

The Young Vic relies on the generous support of many trusts, companies, and individuals to continue our work, on and off stage, year on year.

For their recent support we thank

Public Funders
Arts Council England
Department for Children,
Schools and Families
Lambeth Arts
London Councils
Southwark Council

Corporate Founding Partners
London Eye
ITV London
JPMorgan
talkbackTHAMES

Corporate Supporters
3i
American Airlines
Arts & Business
Bloomberg
Cadbury Schweppes Foundation
E*TRADE Financial
KPMG Foundation
London Communications Agency
Metro
Pali International

The Directors' Circle

Big Cheeses
Bloomberg
HgCapital
Ingenious Media Plc
Land Securities
Thomson Financial

Hot Shots
BC Partners
Royal Bank of Scotland
Slaughter and May
Symbian

Trust Supporters
City Parochial Foundation
Equitable Charitable Trust
Fishmongers' Company
Genesis Foundation
Goethe-Institut
Help a London Child
Hambro Foundation
Institut Francais du Royaume Uni
Jerwood Charitable Foundation
John Thaw Foundation
Lord and Lady Lurgan Trust
Martin Bowley Charitable Trust
Paul Hamlyn Foundation
Peter Minet Trust
Peter Moores Foundation
Pidem Fund
Quercus Charitable Trust
William Howell Fund

Friends of the Young Vic

Production Supporters
Tony & Gisela Bloom
Chris & Jane Lucas
Nadine Majaro & Roger Pilgrim
The Robey Girls
Leo & Susan van der Linden
Anda & Bill Winters

Best Friends
Tom & Sara Attwood
Chris & Frances Bates
Alex & Angela Bernstein
Katie Bradford
Conway van Gelder Grant
The Fairtlough Family
Sarah Hall
Richard Hardman & Family
Nik Holttum & Helen Brannigan
Suzanne & Michael Johnson
Tom Keatinge
John Kinder & Gerry Downey
Simon & Midge Palley
Charles & Donna Scott
Justin Shinebourne
Richard & Julie Slater
Jack & Joanne Tracy
Edgar & Judith Wallner

Great Friends
James & Aundrea Amine
Jane Attias
Angus Aynsley &
Miel de Botton Aynsley
Hilary Brodsky
Rob Brooks
Eddie & Philly Codrington
Robyn Durie
Maureen Elton
Sheila & John Harvey
Sir Robin Jacob
Roger Lloyd Pack
Tony Mackintosh
Ian McKellen
Barbara Minto
Frank & Helen Neale
Georgia Oetker
Anthony & Sally Salz
Dasha Shenkman
Charlotte Stevenson
Rob Wallace

INGENIθUS is proud to continue its creative partnership with the Young Vic supporting another season of exciting theatre.

The Good Soul of Szechuan

The Santa Monica Version

The version of *Der gute Mensch von Sezuan* which is presented here is not just a lively new translation of the familiar text, but a significantly different version of the play, prepared by Brecht himself but previously unpublished in any language. David Harrower's text is based on a 'literal' translation (by Laura Gribble) of a typescript in the Brecht Archive dated 1943 and labelled 'only copy'. This is the script sometimes known as the Santa Monica version.

The more familiar version of the play had been completed back in January 1941 in Finland. Brecht hesitated, but it was this version that eventually came to the theatre in Zurich in February 1943. But Brecht seldom thought of his plays as finished, and he welcomed each new production or publication as an opportunity to rework his material and to produce something better tuned to the new historical and local circumstances. So, now in California, he also embarked on a major rewrite, possibly with a production on Broadway in mind.

Two scenes and half-a-dozen characters were dropped, and the text, which he himself acknowledged was overlong and full of difficulties, was radically shortened. He also undertook a serious change to the plot: the sacks which the family leave with Shen Te in the opening scene transpire to contain not tobacco (as in the familiar version) but opium. From this it follows that Shen Te/Shui Ta becomes involved in an explicitly illegal and destructive (and not merely immoral) trade. Sun eventually becomes a broken-down opium addict. Whether this is a gain or not depends upon one's reading of the play. (A fuller account of the genesis and of the differences between the versions is to be found in the Methuen Drama volume *Brecht Collected Plays: Six*, edited and introduced by John Willett and Ralph Manheim, especially in the Notes, pages 336–51.)

The present text deviates from the Santa Monica script in one respect, namely that one of the lost scenes, the wonderful comic wedding scene, is restored.

One way and another, after that Zurich production and in the course of a number of productions in the States, Austria and West Germany in the late 1940s and early 1950s, it was the earlier version which became the authorised standard. It was the 1941 text which received its East German premiere in 1956 (just six months before Brecht's death) under the direction of Brecht's protégé Benno Besson, and which formed the basis for the first and all subsequent publications in German.

The Santa Monica version was given its first production in 1977 at the Greenwich Theatre, directed by David Thompson, and since then has led a somewhat clandestine life in the theatres of the UK, without ever coming to publication. It is a particular pleasure to be able to present this tougher, tighter, possibly more 'American' version to the reading public. As Brecht commented in his *Journal* (30 June 1940), 'only the stage can decide between possible variants'.

Tom Kuhn,
General Editor

Characters

Shen Te / Shui Ta
First God
Second God
Third God
Wang
Mrs Shin
Carpenter
Nephew
Wife
Father
Policeman
Priest
Agent
Mr Shu Fu
Yang Sun
Mrs Mi Tsu
Mrs Yang

Prelude

A street in the capital of Szechuan province.

Wang   I'm a water seller here in the capital of Szechuan province. It's hard work. When water's scarce, I have to travel miles to fetch it. When there's plenty, I make no money at all. Poverty's the rule in this province. People are saying it's gotten so bad only the Gods can help us now. So imagine my elation when I get told by a cattle dealer who travels around a lot that some very senior Gods have set out on a journey and could well be passing through Szechuan any day now. Apparently, it's 'cause Heaven's alarmed by the amount of complaints it's been getting.

I've been watching for them for three days now, here on the edge of the city, always as night falls, hoping I'll be the first to welcome them. 'Cause you can be sure I won't get a look-in later – they'll be mobbed, with the powerful first in line. I just hope I recognise them. They may not all arrive together, though – they could turn up one at a time so as not to attract attention.

He looks over at some workers passing by.

That can't be them. They're just knocking off work. Look how bent their shoulders are from carrying heavy loads all day. And him over there, he's no God, not with ink on his fingers. No, I'd say he's an office worker at the local cement factory.

Two gentleman walk past.

And these two fine gentlemen – no way they're Gods. Their faces are too sadistic, like men who beat others to get their way, which Gods don't need to do. Over there, those three . . . Now we're talking. They're well fed and look like they've never worked for a living – and there's dust on their shoes – they've travelled many miles. It is them! O Divinities, I'm Wang, the water seller, at your service.

He throws himself to the ground.

First God (*delighted*)   Have you been expecting us?

Wang (*offers them water from his cup*)   For a while now. I knew you'd come, I knew it!

First God   We need a room for the night. Is one available?

Wang   One? We've hundreds of rooms! Divinities, the whole city's at your command. Just tell me whereabouts you want to stay?

The **Gods** *exchange meaningful looks.*

First God   The nearest house, my son. Ask at the nearest one first.

Wang   Only worry is . . . the powerful people round here might find out I chose one of them over another. There's not many can help a man like me, but there's plenty who can harm me.

First God   We'll make it an order then – nearest house first.

Wang   That's Mr Fo's over there!

He hurries over to the house, knocks. The door opens, but then he's turned away. Comes back hesitantly.

No luck. Mr Fo's not home and his servants won't do anything without his say-so – he's very strict. Tell you what though, he'll be fuming when he finds out who they've turned away.

Gods (*smiling*)   I'm sure he will.

Wang   Just a moment. The widow Su lives next door. She'll be over the moon.

He runs over, but is clearly turned away from there too.

I'm going to ask over here. She says she's only got a tiny room which isn't ready and hasn't been cleaned and . . . I can understand her embarrassment. So, next up, Mr Cheng.

Second God   A small room is enough for us. Tell her we are on our way.

Wang   It'll be a mess. Crawling with spiders.

Second God   No matter. More spiders, fewer flies.

Third God   Try Mr Cheng or somewhere else. I don't get on too well with spiders.

Wang *knocks on another door and is let in.*

Voice (*within*)   Gods? Don't come to us with your Gods! We've other things to worry about.

Wang (*returns*)   He's inconsolable, Mr Cheng, inconsolable. He has all his relatives staying and can't bring himself to tell you face to face. I think it's 'cause some of them aren't exactly upstanding, if you know what I mean. He's afraid of your judgement.

Third God   Are we so terrifying?

Wang   Only to bad people. Like them in Kwan province – they've had floods there for years now.

Second God   And why is that do you think?

Wang   'Cause they've got no respect for the Gods.

Second God   Rubbish. It's because they never repair their dam.

First God   Ssst. (*To* **Wang**.) Do you still have hope, my son?

Wang   How can you ask that? Any house here'll have a room for you. People are clamouring to put you up. Just had bad luck so far. Watch this.

He goes, hesitantly, then stops and stands in the street, undecided which house to go to.

Second God   What did I tell you?

Third God   More bad luck . . .

Second God   Bad luck in Shun, bad luck in Kwan and now bad luck in Szechuan. The truth is, the people are no longer God-fearing. Face it, our mission here has failed.

First God   We might find good people at any moment. We can't give up this easily.

Third God   The ruling stated: if enough good people are found who live a moral life, the world can stay as it is. We've found the water seller, haven't we?

He approaches **Wang**, *who's still standing undecided.*

Second God   Wait. When he offered us water, I saw something. Look at his measuring cup.

He shows it to the **First God**.

First God   It has a false bottom.

Second God   He's a cheat.

First God   All right. He fails too. So, he's corrupt – we'll find plenty of other good people. We have to! For two thousand years people have claimed that the world can't go on as it is; that no one can remain virtuous in it. We must search harder for people who are able to live by our commands.

Third God (*to* **Wang**)   Perhaps a room will be too hard to find?

Wang   Not for you! What're you talking about? I'm the one to blame, I should've found you one immediately, I've been slacking.

Third God   It's not your fault.

He goes back to the other **Gods**.

Wang   They can see what's going on. (*Addresses a passing gentleman.*) Excuse me, sir, but three of the highest Gods, whose visit has been the talk of Szechuan for years, have just arrived and are seeking lodgings. Don't walk on . . . Quick, before someone else snaps them up. This is your chance, the chance of a lifetime.

The first gentleman walks off. **Wang** *turns to another.*

Wang   Sir, you heard me. Do you perhaps have a spare room? Doesn't have to be palatial, it's the gesture that counts.

Gentleman   How do I know what kind of Gods they are? Who knows who I'd be letting into my home.

He goes into a tobacconist's. **Wang** *returns to the* **Gods**.

Wang   I've found a gentleman who's definitely certain to say yes.

He sees his cup on the ground, looks uncertainly at the **Gods**, *picks it up and runs back.*

First God   Doesn't sound too encouraging.

Wang (*to the* **Gentleman**, *as he exits shop*)   What about the room then?

Gentleman   How do you know I'm not looking for a room myself?

First God   He's not going to find anything. Szechuan's just like the rest of them.

Wang   These are Principal Gods! Three of them! There's statues of them in the temple if you don't believe me.

Gentleman (*laughs*)   How do I know they're not a bunch of crooks?

He exits.

Wang (*calls after him*)   Where's your respect, you chinless git! You're going to burn in eternity, y'know! The Gods'll shit on you. Your grandkids' grandkids will still be paying for your mistake. You've brought shame on the whole of Szechuan. (*Pause.*) Now only Shen Te's left. Shen Te the hooker. She never says no to anyone. Shen Te!

Shen Te's *head appears at an upstairs window.*

Wang   They're here, the Gods are here, but I can't find any room for them. Can you put them up for the night?

Shen Te   I can't, Wang. I've got a client coming. You can't find anywhere for them at all?

Wang   Nope. Szechuan's a pile of shit.

Shen Te   I could hide when he arrives and he might go away. He's coming to take me out somewhere.

Wang   Can we come up for now?

Shen Te   As long as you're quiet. Can I be straight with them?

Wang   No! They mustn't find out. It's better we wait downstairs. But don't go anywhere with your client, all right?

Shen Te   I'm skint, Wang, and I'm going to be evicted if I don't come up with my rent by tomorrow.

Wang   How can you think about money at a time like this?

Shen Te   Even on the Emperor's birthday, my stomach rumbles. Go on then, I'll take them in.

She turns the light down. The **Gods** *move nearer to* **Wang**.

First God   It's hopeless, isn't it?

Wang (*startled to find the* **Gods** *behind him*)   No, I've found you something.

He wipes his brow.

Gods   Really? Let's see it then.

Wang   No hurry. Relax. The room's being made up.

Third God   We'll sit down and wait then.

Wang   Bit busy here though, eh? All the toing and froing. We're better over there, don't you think?

Second God   We like to watch people. It's why we're here.

Wang   Windy too.

Second God   We can put up with that.

Wang   How about a night-time tour of Szechuan?

Third God   We've walked far enough today. (*Smiles.*) If you want us to move away from here, you just have to say so. (*They walk back.*) Is this all right for you?

They sit on the front steps of a house. **Wang** *sits to one side, on the ground.*

Wang   You'll be staying with a young woman who . . . who lives on her own. She's a good soul – the best person there is in Szechuan.

Third God   We're glad to hear it.

Wang (*to the audience*)   When I picked up my cup just now, they all looked at me funny. D'you think they know? I can't look any of them in the eye.

Third God   You're exhausted.

Wang   A bit. All the rushing around.

First God   Is life hard for the people here?

Wang   Yes. For the good ones.

First God (*penetratingly*)   And for you?

Wang   I know what you're saying. No, I'm not good. But life's not easy for me either.

The **Client** *has arrived at* **Shen Te***'s house. He whistles several times. Each time he does,* **Wang** *flinches.*

Third God   I think he's gone now.

Wang (*at sixes and sevens*)   Yes, sir.

He gets up and walks to the square, leaving behind his carrying pole.

In the meantime, **Shen Te** *has come out of her house to call quietly for* **Wang***. She goes down the street looking for him. So when* **Wang** *now calls for her, there's no answer.*

Wang   She's gone. Left me in the lurch. Off to earn her bloody rent and now there's nowhere for the Gods. They're tired and they're tired of hanging around. What'm I going to say? There's always my own place in the sewage pipe, but, no, I can't take them there. They won't want to stay with me after what happened with the drinking cup. I'm not going back to them, I can't. But my carrying pole's over there . . . What'll I do? I'm leaving it – I'm getting out of Szechuan. I'm going to hide somewhere where they won't find me. I've failed them, the Gods I worship and revere, I've failed them.

He runs off. As soon as he's gone, **Shen Te** *returns. She sees the* **Gods***.*

Shen Te   Are you the Gods? I'm Shen Te. I'd be honoured if you'd accept my invitation to stay in my room for the night.

Third God   Where has the water seller gone?

Shen Te   I must've just missed him.

First God   He probably thought you'd left him and couldn't face us.

Third God (*picks up* **Wang**'s *stuff*)   We'll store this in your house. He'll need it later.

Shen Te *leads them into the house.*

It gets dark, then light again.

Dawn. The **Gods** *step outside to leave, led by* **Shen Te***, who lights their way with a lamp.*

First God   My dear Shen Te, thank you for your hospitality. We won't forget it was you who took us in. Give the water seller his carrying pole back and tell him we're grateful to him for showing us a good person.

Shen Te   I'm not good. When Wang asked me, I hesitated, I wasn't sure.

First God   That doesn't matter – you made the right decision in the end. And truth be told, you gave us more than shelter for the night. There are many – even some of us Gods – who doubt there are any good people left. This is the reason for our journey. We can continue now, happy in the knowledge that we found such a good soul in Szechuan. Goodbye.

Shen Te Wait, Divinities . . . How am I good, tell me? I want to be but every month there's the rent to pay. I sell my body in order to live. And even then I don't make enough, since there are so many others doing it too. I want to follow your commands of brotherly love and honesty, I do, and not covet my neighbour's house and to love one man faithfully and loyally and not exploit anyone or benefit from their misery or rob the poor and the helpless. But how'm I supposed to do all that? Even when I try my best I end up breaking half of them.

First God These are nothing but the worries of every good person.

Third God Farewell, Shen Te. Give my regards to the water seller. He was a good friend to us.

Second God For all the good it's done him.

Third God Take care of yourself.

First God Above all, be good, Shen Te. Goodbye.

They turn to go, already waving goodbye.

Shen Te (*fearful*) But how can I when everything's so expensive?

Second God We can't help you there, I'm afraid. We don't get involved in economic matters.

Third God Wait a moment. If she had a bit more money, surely she'd have a better chance of staying good.

Second God We can't give her anything. We'd have to answer for it up there.

First God So?

They discuss it animatedly.

First God (*to* **Shen Te**, *embarrassed*) We know you're struggling with your rent. We're not poor and so we'll leave something for our accommodation.

Gives her some money.

But you can't tell anyone. It might be misinterpreted.

Second God   *Wildly* misinterpreted.

Third God   No, we're allowed. We're simply paying for our night's lodgings. Nothing in the ruling forbids it. Goodbye then.

They leave hurriedly.

One

A small tobacco shop, not open for business yet, the shelves not completely stocked.

Shen Te (*to the audience*)   It's three days now since the Gods left. The money they left me was more than a thousand silver dollars. So I bought this tobacco shop with it. I moved in yesterday and I hope I can do a lot of good here. Mrs Shin, for example, who I bought the shop from – she came by yesterday to ask for some rice for her kids and I was able to give her some. That's her there, walking across the square again, carrying her bowl.

Mrs Shin *enters. The women bow to one another.*

Shen Te   Good day, Mrs Shin.

Mrs Shin   Good day, Shen Te. How are you finding your new home?

Shen Te   I like it very much. How are your children?

Mrs Shin   Oh, they're living in someone else's house, if you can call that shack a house . . . The littlest one's got a terrible cough already.

Shen Te   That's awful.

Mrs Shin   What would you know about awful? You're doing all right. But running this dump will teach you a thing or two. This neighbourhood's a slum.

Shen Te   But you told me the workers from the cement factory come in here every lunchtime for tobacco.

Mrs Shin   Some of them do. They're the only ones who buy anything. You won't get any locals parting with their money.

Shen Te   You didn't tell me that when you sold me the shop.

Mrs Shin   Don't start accusing me after you've stolen a home from me and my kids. And then you go calling it a shack and a slum! You've got some nerve. (*She cries.*)

Shen Te (*quickly*)   I'll get the rice.

Mrs Shin   I want to borrow some money off you as well.

Shen Te (*while she pours rice into a bowl*)   I can't. I haven't sold anything yet.

Mrs Shin   But I need it. What'm I going to live on? You've taken everything from me. You've got your hands round my throat, choking the life out of me. I'll leave my motherless kids on your doorstep, you tight-fisted hag.

She grabs the bowl of rice from **Shen Te.**

Shen Te   Don't get so angry. You'll spill the rice.

The **Wife** *and* **Husband** *enter, along with their shabbily dressed* **Nephew**. *All carry sacks over their shoulders.*

Wife   My dear Shen Te, we'd heard how well you're doing. Look at you, a businesswoman now. Us, we've nowhere to live at the moment. Our tobacco shop went bust. We wondered if we could stay a night with you? Have you met my nephew? He came along too, he goes everywhere with us.

Nephew (*looking around*)   Nice shop you've got here.

Mrs Shin   Who's this then?

Shen Te   They were my first landlords when I came to the city from the country. (*To the audience.*) When my small bit of money had gone they turned me out onto the street. They'll be afraid now that I'll do the same.

They're poor.
They're homeless.
They've no friends.
How could anyone turn them away?

(*Warmly, to them.*) You're welcome. I'd be glad to put you up. All I have though is a small room at the back of the shop.

Husband   Don't worry. That'll do us.

Wife (*while* **Shen Te** *brings in tea*)   Best we just settle in and not get in your way. I suppose you chose a tobacco shop because it reminded you of your first home in the city, eh? We can pass on a few tips. Bet you're glad we came now.

Mrs Shin (*sarcastically*)   She'll be even gladder if a few paying customers come as well.

Wife   Is that a dig at us?

Husband   Shhh. She's got a customer.

An **Unemployed Man** *enters.*

Unemployed Man   Hello. I'm unemployed.

Mrs Shin *laughs.*

Shen Te   What can I do for you?

Unemployed Man   I heard you're opening tomorrow so I thought to myself, she'll be unpacking stuff, and usually some of it falls out and gets damaged. Ciggies, y'know, stuff like that? Any chance of one?

Wife   He's got a nerve, begging for tobacco. Bread, I'd understand . . .

Unemployed Man   Bread's expensive. All I want's a couple of puffs on a cigarette and I'll be a new man. Right now, I'm a wreck.

Shen Te (*gives him cigarettes*)   It's important to feel like a new man. You're my first customer and you're going to bring me luck.

The **Unemployed Man** *lights up, inhales and exits, coughing.*

Wife   Was that wise, dear Shen Te?

Mrs Shin   If that's how you're going to trade, you'll be out of business in three days.

Husband   I bet you he had money on him.

Shen Te   He said he had nothing.

Nephew   How do you know he wasn't lying?

Shen Te (*angry*)   How do I know he was?

Wife (*shakes her head*)   She can't say no. You're too good, Shen Te. If you want to hold on to your shop, you'll have to learn to refuse people.

Husband   Why don't you tell people the shop's not yours? Say it belongs to a relative – a cousin or something.

Mrs Shin   She'd never do that, she's too intent on do-gooding.

Shen Te (*laughs*)   Just keep the complaints coming. I'll turf you lot out and take my rice back.

Wife (*outraged*)   You give her rice as well?

Shen Te (*to the audience*)
    They're bad people.
    They don't trust anyone.
    They even begrudge someone a bowl of rice.
    They want to grab everything for themselves.
    Who could blame them?

A little man, the **Carpenter,** *enters.* **Mrs Shin** *gets up hastily to go.*

Mrs Shin   I'll drop in again tomorrow.

She exits.

Carpenter   Stop, Mrs Shin, it's you I came to see.

Wife   Does she come often then? She got some kind of claim on you?

Shen Te   No. But she's hungry.

Carpenter   She knows why she's running. You the new owner? I see you're stocking the shelves – shelves that aren't yours. Not unless you pay for them. The scum that were here before you never did. (*To the others.*) I'm the carpenter, Lin To.

Shen Te   I thought everything was included in the price.

Carpenter   Robbery. Robbery and fraud. I bet you and that Mrs Shin are in this together. I want fifty silver dollars for the work I did.

Shen Te   How can I pay you? I haven't made any money yet.

Carpenter   Then I'll have all your assets sold off. Immediately. So pay up or be sold off, your choice.

Husband (*prompting* **Shen Te**)   Tell him . . . you'll have to consult your cousin . . .

Shen Te   Can't it wait till next month?

Carpenter (*shouting*)   No!

Shen Te   Do you have to be so hard-nosed, Mr Lin To? I can't meet everyone's demands.

(*To the audience.*)
   A little leniency and one's strength doubles.
   A carthorse stops to chew a tuft of grass,
   Leave him to it and he'll pull better than before.
   Show a bit of patience in June and come August the peach
      tree will be weighed down with fruit.
   Without forbearance how can we live together?
   Allow a small delay
   And the furthest destinations are easily reached.

(*To the* **Carpenter**.) That's all I'm asking for, Mr Lin To.

Carpenter   And who'll be patient with me and my family?

He pulls a shelf from the wall.

Pay up or I take my shelves with me.

Wife   Shen Te, why don't you let your cousin take care of the matter . . . ? (*To the* **Carpenter**.) Write an invoice and her cousin'll pay you.

Carpenter   I've heard about cousins like that.

Nephew   Don't laugh. I know him personally.

Husband   He's got a sharp brain. He knows what's what.

Carpenter (*to* **Shen Te**)   I hope for your sake he does. All right, I'll write him an invoice.

He turns the shelf upside down, sits on it and writes out an invoice.

Wife (*to* **Shen Te**)   He'll fleece you for those few planks if you don't put a stop to it. Don't ever accept a demand, you hear, however justified, 'cause then you'll be inundated with others. Throw a bone in the garbage and before you know it all the dogs in the neighbourhood are in your yard fighting over it. What do you think the courts are there for?

Shen Te   The courts won't feed him if his labour doesn't. He wants to be paid for the work he's done. He has a family to support. I feel awful that I can't pay him. What will the Gods say?

Husband   You did enough taking us in.

A limping man, the **Brother**, *and a pregnant woman, the* **Sister-in-Law**, *enter.*

Brother (*to the couple*)   So this's where you've got to. My own flesh and blood leave us abandoned on a street corner.

Wife (*to* **Shen Te**, *embarrassed*)   This is my brother Wung and my sister-in-law. (*To both of them.*) Sit down and keep quiet so you don't bother our old friend, Miss Shen Te. You can stay here, it's fine by her. (*To* **Shen Te**.) I think we'll have to take both of them in. My sister-in-law's five months gone. It's only right, isn't it?

Shen Te   They're both welcome.

Wife   Say thank you. There's cups back there. (*To* **Shen Te**.) They've nowhere else to go. Lucky for them you bought this shop.

Carpenter (*grumpily*)   My bill. I'll be back here first thing tomorrow.

He leaves.

Nephew (*calls after him*)   Don't you worry, her cousin'll pay you.

Sister-in-Law (*quietly, to the* **Nephew**)   Things won't last like this too long.

An old man, **Grandfather***, enters led by a* **Boy**.

Boy   Here they are.

Wife   Hello, Grandfather. (*To* **Shen Te**.) He'll have been worried about us. And the boy, hasn't he grown? He eats like a wolf. Who else you got with you?

Husband (*looking around*)   Only your niece.

A young girl, the **Niece***, enters.*

Sister-in-Law (*quietly to the* **Nephew**)   Told you. The rats are boarding the sinking ship . . .

Wife (*to* **Shen Te**)   She's a young relative of mine from the country. That'll be it now. There weren't this many of us when you lived with us before, were there? We've just multiplied. The worse off we got, the more of us appeared. And the more of us there were, the worse off we got. Better lock up now in case the ranks swell again.

She locks up and everyone sits down.

The important thing is we don't disturb your business, so we've planned it like this: the younger ones will go out during the day leaving Grandfather, sister-in-law and perhaps me as well. The rest of them will only drop in once or twice a day, all right?

Nephew (*jokily, to* **Shen Te**)   Just hope your cousin doesn't turn up in the night.

Sister-in-Law *laughs.*

Brother (*helps himself to a cigarette*)   Don't mind us smoking the odd one, do you?

Husband   Course she doesn't.

Everyone takes a cigarette. The **Brother** *passes a jug of wine around.*

Nephew   Drink up. It's on her cousin.

Grandfather (*to* **Shen Te**)   Good day.

Shen Te *is confused by the delayed greeting. She bows. Still in her hand, the* **Carpenter**'s *bill.*

Wife   Is no one going to sing for our kind hostess?

Nephew   Grandad can start.

They sing 'The Smoke Song'.

Grandfather
> Before my hair went grey I used to think
> My brains were all I needed to survive,
> But if there's nothing in my house to eat or drink,
> How can pure intellect keep me alive?
> > That's why I say: stuff it!
> > Just like grey smoke
> > Fading in cold air.
> > That's how you'll go too.

Husband
> Hard work and honesty get you nowhere.
> I know that's why I took the crooked way.
> But even that leads only to failure,
> So I've got sod all else to say.
> > Except to say: stuff it!
> > Just like grey smoke
> > Fading in cold air.
> > No one will remember you.

Niece

I hear the old folk say there is no hope,
Any dreams you have Time cuts them short
If you're young like me life's door is wide open
But I'm pretty sure it leads to nowt.
    And so I also say: stuff it!
    Just like grey smoke
    Fading in cold air,
    You will vanish for ever.

Nephew   Where's the wine from?

Sister-in-Law (*points to* **Brother**)   He sold some of that special tobacco for it.

Husband   You did what? You bastard, we said we'd never dip into it, even when we had nowhere to stay.

Brother   Bugger off, you – my wife was freezing. Don't bloody drink the wine then. Give me that jug!

They scuffle. The tobacco shelves fall over.

Shen Te (*imploringly*)   Watch it! This is my shop! It was a gift of the Gods. Take whatever you want, but don't wreck it.

Wife   This place is smaller than I thought. I shouldn't have told Auntie and others about it, should I? If they come we'll be crammed in here.

Sister-in-Law (*about* **Shen Te**)   Her face is dropping as well, you noticed?

Voices outside. A knock on the door.

Voice   Open up. It's us.

Wife   Oh, is that you, Auntie? What're we going to do?

Shen Te   My beautiful shop. My shop that was full of hope. I've not even opened yet and already it's chaos.

(*To the audience.*)
    This little lifeboat of salvation

Is being sucked down into the deep.
Too many of the shipwrecked
Are desperately reaching out for it.

Interlude

Under a bridge.

Wang *the water seller crouching on the riverbank.*

Wang (*looking around*)   All's quiet. I've been hiding for four days now. They won't find me – I'm keeping my eyes peeled. I did the smart thing and ran in the direction they were heading. On the second day they passed over the bridge. I heard their steps above me. Now they'll be far away, which means I'm safe from them.

He leans back, falls asleep. Music. The bank becomes transparent and the **Gods** *appear.* **Wang** *lifts his arm to cover himself as if about to be struck.*

Wang   All right, I know – I failed you. I couldn't find anyone who'd give you a room for the night. Go. Leave me alone.

First God   No, you did find someone. She took us in and watched over us as we slept, and in the morning, as we were leaving, she lit our way with a lamp. You found our good person for us, a good soul of Szechuan.

Wang   Shen Te?

Third God   Of course.

Wang   And I ran off showing no faith in her. I thought she was only thinking about her rent and wouldn't come back.

Gods
O you weak man,
Well meaning but weak man.
Where there is hardship you think there can be no goodness.
Where there is risk you believe there will be no bravery,

Such weakness which sees no virtue in anyone.
O rash judgement, O thoughtless desperation.

Wang   Divinities, I'm so ashamed.

First God   Water seller, we want you to go to Szechuan and
report back to us about all the good Shen Te is doing. Things
are going well for her. She's bought a small shop with some
money she was given – so she can do what her kind heart bids
her. You must stand by her and encourage her – that is what
the good deserve. We, meanwhile, will carry on with our
journey and put an end finally to the belief that good people
cannot survive on this earth.

Two

The tobacco shop.

*Sleeping people lie everywhere. The lamp still burns. A knock on the door.
The* **Wife** *raises herself up, still half asleep.*

Wife   Shen Te, someone's at the door. Where is she?

Nephew   Probably making breakfast for her cousin. He'll
want to eat before he starts sorting out this mess.

The **Wife** *laughs and shuffles to the door. A young man,* **Shui Ta,**
enters. Behind him, the **Carpenter**.

Shui Ta   I'm the cousin.

Wife (*taken aback*)   You what?

Shui Ta   Call me Shui Ta.

Guests (*rousing each other*)   It's the cousin . . . ! / But that was
a joke. / She doesn't have a cousin. / There's someone here
saying he's the cousin. / No, no way!

Nephew   If you're her cousin, mister, then you can go and
help Shen Te make breakfast. Go on. Chop chop.

Shui Ta (*extinguishes the lamp*)   This is my shop, not a bloody
refuge! Get dressed, all of you. Now!

Husband   *Your* shop? I thought it was Shen Te's.

Shui Ta *shakes his head.*

Husband   It's not?

Sister-in-Law   She was lying to us. Where is she, anyway?

Shui Ta   She's attending to other business, so I'm giving the orders now – no more charity, no more helping hand.

Wife (*shaken*)   And we thought she was a good person . . .

Nephew (*to* **Shui Ta**)   I don't believe you. Start looking for her.

Husband   Yes, c'mon – you, you and you, get looking. We'll stay here with Grandfather and hold the fort. The boy can go and find us something to eat. (*To the* **Boy**.) See that pastry shop on the corner? Get over there and fill your pockets.

Sister-in-Law   And bring me back a couple of those little white cakes.

Husband   Make sure the baker doesn't see you. And keep clear of the copper.

The **Boy** *nods, goes. The others get dressed.*

Shui Ta   I don't want any thieving connected with this shop.

Nephew   Don't worry about him, Shen Te'll sort him out.

The **Nephew**, **Brother**, **Sister-in-Law** *and* **Niece** *exit.*

Sister-in-Law   Save some food for us.

Shui Ta (*calmly*)   They won't find her. And by the way, my cousin's hospitality towards you has now ended. There's far too many of you. I want this shop to be run like a shop.

Husband   Shen Te wouldn't do this to us.

Shui Ta   Well then, Shen Te needs to learn, doesn't she? (*To the* **Carpenter**.) This city's in crisis. It's beyond help – no one can change anything here. Someone wrote a poem eleven hundred years ago and things are still the same as then:

When the Governor was asked what was needed
To help the city's freezing poor, he replied,
'A blanket ten thousand feet long
To cover the suburbs.'

He starts clearing up the shop.

Carpenter   Your cousin owes me for the shelves. Fifty silver dollars.

Shui Ta (*takes out money*)   You don't think fifty's too steep?

Carpenter   Nope. And I don't do discounts. Wife and kids to feed.

Shui Ta   How many?

Carpenter   Four.

Shui Ta   Then I'll give you five silver dollars.

Carpenter (*laughs*)   Funny guy. Those shelves are walnut.

Shui Ta   Take them down then.

Carpenter   What d'you mean?

Shui Ta   They're too expensive. Take them down.

Wife   That's telling him. (*She laughs.*)

Carpenter   I want Miss Shen Te brought here. She'll listen to me.

Shui Ta   Of course she will. That's why she's facing ruin.

Carpenter (*resolutely takes a shelf, carries it to the door*)   All right, you can stack all your tobacco and stuff on the floor. See if I care.

Shui Ta (*to the* **Husband**)   Don't just stand there then. Give him a hand.

Husband (*takes another shelf, carries it grinning*)   Watch yourselves, walnut shelves coming through.

Carpenter   You bastard. You want my family to starve?

Shui Ta   All right, I'll offer you two dollars for the lot. You're right, I don't want to my stock lying on the floor.

Carpenter   Five!

Shui Ta *looks calmly out the window. The* **Husband** *busies himself carrying the shelves outside.*

Carpenter   Watch what you're doing, idiot. (*Desperately.*) They were made to measure. They fit this wall and nowhere else. I cut those planks special, mister.

Shui Ta   That's why I'm offering two dollars. You cut down the wood, I cut down the price.

The **Wife** *squeals with pleasure.*

Carpenter   I'm sick of this. Keep the bloody shelves, pay me whatever you've got.

Shui Ta   Two silver dollars.

He puts the coins on the table. The **Carpenter** *takes them. The* **Husband** *starts carrying the planks back inside.*

Husband   That's not bad for a pile of planks.

Carpenter   It better be enough to get me pissed.

He exits.

Husband   Oh, we got him good.

Wife (*wiping tears of laughter away*)   'They're walnut.' 'Take them down.' 'Fifty silver dollars.' That's how you deal with people like him.

Shui Ta   'That's how you deal with people like him.' I want you two out of here now.

Husband   Us? Why?

Shui Ta   Because you're thieves and parasites. Now! And no arguing or pleading.

Husband   Don't say anything. It's not good to get angry on an empty stomach. Where's that bloody boy got to?

Shui Ta   I've already told you – he doesn't come through that door with stolen cakes! (*Shouts suddenly.*) Get out! (*They stay seated. Calmly.*) So be it.

*He goes to the door and greets someone outside. A **Policeman** appears at the door.*

Shui Ta   I take it this is your neighbourhood, Officer.

Policeman   Correct, sir.

Shui Ta   The name's Shui Ta. (*They smile.*) Lovely weather we're having.

Policeman   A little too warm, perhaps.

Shui Ta   Maybe a little.

Husband (*quietly to the **Wife***)   If the boy comes back we'll get it.

*He surreptitiously tries to signal to **Shui Ta**, who ignores him.*

Shui Ta   I suppose it all depends whether you're standing in a cool place or outside on a hot, dusty street.

Policeman   I suppose it does.

Wife (*to the **Husband***)   Calm down. The boy's not stupid. He'll stay away if he sees a policeman in the doorway.

Shui Ta   Why don't you come in? The shop belongs to me and my cousin, and let me assure you we consider it imperative to be on good terms with the authorities.

Policeman (*coming in*)   Very kind of you, Mr Shui Ta. Yes, it certainly is cooler in here.

Husband (*quietly*)   He's doing it on purpose now. The boy won't see him.

Shui Ta   They're visitors. Distant acquaintances of my cousin's, so I'm told. Only passing through.

They bow to one another.

In fact, we were just saying our goodbyes.

Husband (*hoarsely*)   Yep, that'll be us off then.

Shui Ta   I'll pass your thanks on to my cousin and tell her you're sorry you couldn't stay.

From the street outside, shouts of 'Stop, thief.'

Policeman   What's that?

*The **Boy** arrives, cakes and bread falling from his clothes. The **Wife** signals frantically for him to get out. He turns to run.*

Policeman   Oi, you, stop! (*Grabs him.*) Where did you get these cakes?

Boy   Over there.

Policeman   Stealing, eh?

Wife   We don't know anything about it. I've no idea who he is.

Policeman   Do you have an explanation, Mr Shui Ta?

Shui Ta *is silent.*

Policeman   All right, we'll all go down to the police station then.

Shui Ta   Officer, I am shocked that something like this could happen here.

Wife (*points at **Shui Ta***)   He knew exactly what the boy was up to!

Shui Ta   If I did, Officer, I'd hardly have invited you in here, would I?

Policeman   No. Of course not. I have to take them in for questioning, Mr Shui Ta.

Shui Ta *bows his assent.*

Shui Ta   One last thing before you go. The sacks you brought – are you not taking them with you?

Husband (*imploringly*)   Sacks? What sacks? We didn't bring any sacks.

Shui Ta   Sorry, Officer, my cousin's mistake. A misunderstanding.

Policeman   Right, you lot. Get moving.

He ushers them out.

Grandfather (*solemnly, in the doorway*)   Good day.

Everyone leaves except **Shui Ta**, *who walks to the back of the shop and pulls out a sack. He shows it to the audience.*

Shui Ta   See this? It's heroin.

He hears someone coming, hides the sack.

Policeman   I handed the suspects over to a colleague because I wanted to come back to pass on the gratitude of the city police department.

Shui Ta   No, Officer, it's you who must be thanked.

Policeman (*casually*)   You mentioned earlier something about some sacks. You haven't come across any of them?

Shui Ta   Nothing at all. Do you smoke, Officer?

Policeman (*pocketing two cigars*)   I have to tell you my department wasn't sure about this shop, but your determined stance on the side of the law has shown us that you're a pillar of law and order within the community. You'll be staying on, I hope?

Shui Ta   I can't, unfortunately. I just dropped by to help out my cousin, that's all. I told her she'll have to learn to survive by herself, I won't always be here. Doesn't stop a cousin from worrying about her, though.

Policeman   What about a husband for her?

Shui Ta   A husband?

Policeman (*enthusiastically*)   Why not? She's got a lot going for her. I mean, for instance, there's Mr Shu Fu the barber who lives next door. He owns twelve houses and has only the one wife, who's getting on a bit. Only yesterday, in fact, he expressed to me an interest in the young lady. And he also asked about her financial situation. Now, if that doesn't show genuine feeling . . .

Shui Ta (*cautiously*)   That's not such a bad idea. Could you arrange a meeting?

Policeman   Yes, I think I could probably do that. Course it'd have to be done delicately – Mr Shu Fu is an honourable man. Perhaps they could accidentally meet outside the tea shop near the municipal lake. There's a bath hut nearby. I know because I arrested a vagrant there only last week. Miss Shen Te could be . . . could be admiring the carps in the lake and could, in her appreciation, say . . . say . . .

Shui Ta   'Look at the lovely carps.'

Policeman   Brilliant. And Mr Shu Fu could reply . . .

Shui Ta   'All I see is a beautiful face reflected in the water.'

Policeman   Perfect. I'll go and speak with Mr Shu Fu immediately. You can be sure, Mr Shui Ta, the Szechuan authorities want only the best for the honest businessman.

Shui Ta   To be honest, I thought there was no hope for this business. My cousin believes it was gifted to her by the Gods. But suddenly things have got a lot brighter. Scary, isn't it, that to succeed in life a person needs good fortune, a head full of ideas and plenty of loyal friends.

Three

Dusk in the municipal park.

A young man in torn clothes watches an aeroplane flying high over the park. He's **Yang Sun**.

He takes out a rope, glances around. He's heading over to a large willow tree when two **Prostitutes** *come walking along the path. One is old, the other is the* **Niece** *from the family who descended on* **Shen Te***'s shop.*

Young Prostitute   Hey, you wanting any business, darling?

Yang Sun   Maybe – if you buy me something to eat first.

Old Prostitute   Course we will . . . (*To the* **Young Prostitute**.) You're wasting your time, that's the unemployed pilot.

Young Prostitute   But there's no one else here – and it's going to start raining in a minute.

Old Prostitute   Trust me, you never know what you'll find.

They walk on.

Yang Sun *throws the rope over one of the branches of the willow.*

The two **Prostitutes** *enter again, walking quickly. They don't notice him this time.*

Young Prostitute   I'm telling you it's going to piss down.

Shen Te *comes walking along the path.*

Old Prostitute   Look who it is, the evil pig of Szechuan. I want to have a go at her.

Young Prostitute   It was her cousin, it wasn't her. She took my family in. And she offered to pay for the stolen cakes. I've got nothing against her.

Old Prostitute   Well, I do. (*Loudly.*) If it isn't Shen Te, a filthy rich businesswoman now, but still on the streets stealing customers from us.

Shen Te   I'm not. I'm going to the tea house by the lake.

Young Prostitute   You really marrying that barber who's got three children?

Shen Te (*nods*)   I'm off to meet him now.

Yang Sun   Give me some peace here, will you?

Old Prostitute   You shut your mouth!

The **Prostitutes** *exit.*

Yang Sun (*calls after them*)   Vultures! Vampires! (*To the audience.*) Even in this remote spot, even in the pouring rain, you still find them hunting mercilessly for prey, ready to pick them off and devour them.

Shen Te (*angrily*)   Don't speak about them like that . . . ! (*Notices the rope.*) Oh . . . !

Yang Sun   What?

Shen Te   What's the rope for?

Yang Sun   Get going, sister. Hop it. I've got nothing, nada, not even a nickel. And even if I had, I'd buy a cup of water before I spent it on you.

It starts to rain.

Shen Te   No. Not rope. Don't do it.

Yang Sun   I told you to get lost!

Shen Te   It's raining.

Yang Sun   Don't be trying to come and shelter under this tree.

Shen Te (*standing in the rain*)   No.

Yang Sun   Exactly. No business here. You're too ugly for me anyway. Bandy legs.

Shen Te   No, I haven't.

Yang Sun   All right, I don't need to see them. C'mon then, get out of the rain.

Shen Te *walks over and sits under the tree.*

Shen Te   Why are you doing that?

Yang Sun   To get rid of you. (*Pause.*) D'you know what a mail pilot is?

Shen Te   Yes. I've seen a few of them in the tea house.

Yang Sun   No, you haven't. They weren't pilots. What you saw was a couple of air-headed idiots in leather helmets with no ear for an engine or feel for a machine and who only get to fly because they bribe the hangar manager. Ask one of them to let her bank through the clouds and then pull her ever so gently with the joystick and they'll say, 'Sorry, mate, not in my contract.' They're an obscenity. You land a plane on a runway like it's your own arse you're touching down . . . I'm a real pilot – and a real fucking idiot – know why? 'Cause at flying school in Beijing I read every book they had about flying except for one page – one page that I skipped – the page that said that there's sod-all work for pilots nowadays. So that's what I am – a pilot without a plane. A mail pilot with no mail. You're nodding, but you've no idea what what I'm talking about.

Shen Te   I do.

Yang Sun   No, you don't. You *can't*.

Shen Te (*half laughing, half crying*)   When we were kids we found a bird – a crane with a broken wing. He got so attached to us. We used to play with him and he'd run after us, squawking if we got too far ahead. But then in spring and autumn, when he saw the other birds migrating, flying over our village, he got so restless and distracted. And I knew how he felt.

Yang Sun   Don't cry.

Shen Te   No.

Yang Sun   It's bad for your complexion.

Shen Te   All right, I'm stopping.

Shen Te *wipes her tears away with her sleeve.* **Yang Sun,** *leaning against the tree, not looking at her, reaches out and touches her face.*

Yang Sun   You can't even wipe your face properly.

He wipes it for her with a piece of sackcloth. Pause.

If you're going to stop me from hanging myself, at least you can say something.

Shen Te   I don't know what to say.

Yang Sun   So why d'you want to cut me down, sister?

Shen Te   I'm scared. (*Nods.*) You're only feeling like this 'cause it's such a miserable evening.

(*To the audience.*)
   In our country
   There should be no miserable evenings.
   Or high bridges over rivers.
   Even the hour before dawn breaks
   Or the long, dark winter months
   All of them are laden with danger.
   In the face of such misery
   It takes only the smallest thing
   For people to throw their precious lives away.

Yang Sun   Tell me about yourself then.

Shen Te   There's not much to know. I own a small shop.

Yang Sun   So you're not touting for trade . . .

Shen Te   No. But before that, yes, I was on the street.

Yang Sun   And the shop – I suppose that was a gift from the Gods?

Shen Te   Yes.

Yang Sun   One fine evening they came to you and said: 'Here's some money.'

Shen Te (*quietly laughs*)   One fine morning actually.

Yang Sun   You're not a lot of fun, are you?

Shen Te (*after a pause*)   I can play the zither a bit. And I do impersonations of people. (*With a deep voice she does the impression of a dignitary.*) 'Oh damn and blast it, my dear, I seem to have left my wallet at home.' Then when I got the shop I gave my zither away and told myself, Shen Te, you must apply yourself, you must be disciplined.

   I'm a rich woman now.
   I can do what I want.

I'll sleep on my own
For a whole year.
I'll have nothing to do with men.

Yang Sun   But now you're marrying one? This man you're meeting at the tea house by the lake?

Shen Te's *silent.*

Yang Sun   D'you know anything about love?

Shen Te   Everything there is to know.

Yang Sun   You know nothing. Did you like being in love?

Shen Te   No.

Yang Sun (*strokes her face without looking at her*)   D'you like that?

Shen Te   Yes.

Yang Sun   Easily satisfied, aren't you? What a city!

Shen Te   Don't you have any friends?

Yang Sun   Loads. But none of them want to know I'm still jobless. They look as me as if it's my fault.

Shen Te   They say: to speak without hope is to speak without kindness.

Yang Sun   I have no hope. I'm five hundred silver dollars short of having hope. I got a letter this morning telling me about a job – and five hundred is how much it'll cost me to get that job. So, that's why I say – stuff hope, reach for the rope.

Shen Te   A job as a pilot?

He nods, and she continues slowly.

I have a friend – he's my cousin, actually – who might be able to get his hands on that kind of money. He's very hard-headed, though, and very ruthless. He doesn't lend to just anyone. But you're a pilot and pilots need to fly, he'll understand that.

Yang Sun   What're you going on about?

Shen Te   Come to the tobacco shop in Sandalmakers Lane
tomorrow. If I'm not there, ask for my cousin.

Yang Sun (*laughs*)   And what if no one's there? (*Looks at her.*)
Your shawl's the prettiest thing about you.

Shen Te   I felt a raindrop just then.

Yang Sun   Where?

Shen Te   Between my eyes.

Yang Sun   More towards the right one or the left one?

Shen Te   More towards the left.

Yang Sun   Good. (*After a while, sleepily.*) And you're definitely
through with men?

Shen Te (*smiles*)   My legs are not bandy.

Yang Sun   Maybe not.

Shen Te   Definitely not.

Yang Sun (*leans wearily against the tree*)   But since I haven't
eaten anything for two days, and haven't drunk anything for
one, I couldn't make love to you even if I wanted to.

Shen Te   I like it in the rain.

Wang *arrives and sings 'The Song of the Water Seller in the Rain'.*

Wang
   I sell water, cups of water
   Now of course it's pissing raining
   Walked for miles to fetch this water
   This is how I make my living:
   'Come and buy my fresh, pure water!'
   But no one wants it
   No one pays me
   They're too desperate and greedy
      Buy my water, you bastards!

   Could I stop the sky from leaking
   Halt the rain for seven years

I'd sell water by the drop
'Give us water,' they'd be screaming
Hands were grabbing out for me
But I only gave them water
If the bastards
Had been good to me
Buy my water, you dogs!

(*Laughing.*)
You're happy now gulping the water
On your back, mouths wide open
Sucking on the sky's huge udder
No one bothered what it costs
I'm left shouting: 'Fresh, pure water!'
But no one wants it
No one pays me
They're too desperate and greedy
Buy water, you bastard dogs.

The rain's stopped. **Shen Te** *sees* **Wang** *and walks towards him.*

Shen Te   Wang, you're back. Your carrying pole's at my place.

Wang   Thank you. How are you, Shen Te?

Shen Te   I'm great. I've just met a really smart and exciting man. I'd like to buy a cup of your water.

Wang   Just tilt your head back and open your mouth. You can drink as much water as you want. The willow over there's dripping with it.

Shen Te   But I want your water, Wang.

You've carried it here from far away
Exhausting yourself.
And no one's buying because it's raining today.
I want it for that man over there.
He's a pilot.
Pilots live braver lives than other people.
With only the clouds for company

He weathers the storms
And flies across the heavens
Delivering mail to people in distant parts.

Wang   I thought you're supposed to be meeting someone in the park who can help you.

Shen Te   I've found someone now *I* can help.

She pays for the water, takes it over to **Yang Sun**. *She laughs, calls back to* **Wang**.

Shen Te   He's asleep! We've all tired him out – the rain, his hopelessness, and me.

Interlude

Wang'*s sleeping place in a sewer pipe.*

Wang *asleep. The sewer pipe becomes transparent. He sees the* **Gods** *in his sleep.*

Wang (*excited*)   I saw her, Divinities, I saw Shen Te. She's doing you proud.

First God   We are glad to hear that.

Wang   She's in love! She introduced me to her boyfriend. Things are going so well for her.

First God   Hopefully it is strengthening her endeavours to be good.

Wang   Absolutely. She does as many good deeds as she can.

First God (*keenly*)   Such as . . .

Wang   No one leaves her shop without tobacco, even if they have no money.

First God   That sounds encouraging. What else?

Wang   She took in a family of eight who had nowhere to live.

First God (*triumphantly, to* **Second God**)   Do you hear that? Eight! (*To* **Wang**.) What else has she done?

Wang   She bought a cup of water from me even though it was raining.

First God   Small, kindly acts as well – this is wonderful to hear.

Wang   But it is proving expensive. The shop doesn't bring in much.

First God   A thoughtful gardener can do wonders with the tiniest plot of land.

Wang   She does! Every morning she gives rice to the needy – she must spend half her income on it.

First God (*slightly disappointed*)   I'm not complaining. It's not a bad start at all.

Wang   Remember, times aren't easy. She had to get her cousin's help because her shop was in trouble.

> Hardly was the shelter built
> When out of the wintry sky
> All the bedraggled birds came flying
> Fighting for a place inside
> And the hungry fox
> Gnawed through the thin walls
> And the one-legged wolf
> Knocked over the small bowl of rice.

What I mean is, things had gotten too much for her to cope with on her own. But everyone still talks of how good she is. They call her the 'Angel of the Suburbs'. Everyone except Lin To, the carpenter.

First God   What do you mean? Does the carpenter talk badly of her?

Wang   He still says he hasn't been paid in full for the shelves he built.

Second God   The carpenter wasn't paid? How could Shen Te let that happen?

Wang   She probably didn't have the money.

Second God   It doesn't matter. What is owed must be paid. She cannot let this continue. One must obey the spirit of our commands to the letter.

Wang   It was her cousin, not her.

Second God   Then this cousin must not be allowed into the shop again.

Wang (*dejected*)   I understand you, Divinities. But can I say in Shen Te's defence that her cousin's considered a very reputable businessman. Even the police speak highly of him.

First God   Well, we should not to pass judgement on this cousin without a hearing. I admit I know nothing of business. Perhaps we should find out what normal practice is in such matters. Business! Is it absolutely necessary? It's everywhere nowadays. I mean, did the Seven Benevolent Kings do business? Did Kung the Just sell fish? What does business have to do with a righteous and worthy life?

Second God (*with a very blocked nose*)   Anyhow, it must not be allowed to happen again.

He turns to leave. The other two **Gods** *do likewise.*

Third God (*embarrassed, to* **Wang**)   Excuse our somewhat harsh tone today. We're exhausted; we've hardly slept. The accommodation last night . . . The wealthy direct us towards the poor, but the poor never have enough rooms.

Gods (*departing, grumbling*)   Even the best show weakness. / You can't take anything for granted. / Straight from the heart, yes, but it counts for nothing. / She should at least have . . .

They fade into inaudibility.

Wang (*calls after them*)   Don't be too hard on us! You're maybe expecting too much to begin with.

Four

In front of the curtain.

Shen Te *appears, holding* **Shui Ta***'s mask and suit, and sings 'The Song of the Powerlessness of the Gods and the Good'.*

Shen Te
  In our country
  The able man needs luck
  Only with the right connections
  Is he able to contribute
  The good can do nothing for themselves
  And the Gods have no power to help.

  Why don't the Gods have tanks and cannons
  Battleships, bombers and mines
  To destroy the bad and defend the good?
  Show their support for mankind

  In our country
  The good don't stay good for long
  When our stomachs are empty
  We fight and debase each other
  Oh, the laws of the Gods
  Are no use to the hungry

  Why don't the Gods come to market
  Share out their wealth with a smile
  Their bread and wine would keep us all happy
  Maybe then we'd be friendly and kind

  In our country
  You need the strength of an empire
  Just to put food on the table
  What point in helping a single poor beggar
  If you kick aside everyone else?

  I want to hear the Gods shout from the skies
  That they owe us a better world
  Help to arm us with tanks and rifles
  To march against suffering and want. Take aim! Fire!

Five

The tobacco shop.

Shui Ta's *at the counter, reading the newspaper. He doesn't pay any attention to* **Mrs Shin**, *who's talking while cleaning the shop.*

Mrs Shin   I hate gossip, Mr Shui Ta, but I think you should know what's going on. People are talking about Miss Shen Te staying out until all hours of the morning – plus the local spongers start queuing outside the shop first thing for a plateful of rice. This shop's getting a bad reputation.

When she gets no answer from him, she leaves, carrying her bucket.

Yang Sun (*from outside*)   Is this Miss Shen Te's shop?

Mrs Shin   Yes. But her cousin's there today.

With the light step of **Shen Te**, **Shui Ta** *walks to the mirror and is just about to do up his hair when he notices his error. He turns away with a soft laugh.* **Yang Sun** *enters. Behind him enters* **Mrs Shin**, *curious. She walks past him into the back of the shop.*

Yang Sun   I'm Yang Sun.

Shui Ta *bows.*

Yang Sun   Is Shen Te here?

Shui Ta   No, she's not.

Yang Sun   I expect she's told you about us.

He begins to inspect the shop.

A real shop! I thought she was making it up.

He looks into the little boxes and china pots with satisfaction.

Not bad, not bad at all.

He helps himself to a cigar. **Shui Ta** *lights it.*

Yang Sun   I reckon we could squeeze five hundred out of this, don't you think?

Shui Ta (*surprised, but also amused*)   May I ask, do you intend to sell it immediately?

Yang Sun   D'you see five hundred in cash lying around anywhere?

Shui Ta *shakes his head.*

Yang Sun   So we'll have to sell.

Shui Ta   I'd say she was a bit hasty promising you the money. It could cost her the shop. You know the saying: haste is the wind that blows down the scaffolding.

Yang Sun   I need the money fast or I can forget about the job. And the girl's not one to hang about. That goes for most things with her . . .

Shui Ta   Really?

Yang Sun   Yes, really.

Shui Ta   And can I ask what the money's for?

Yang Sun   You're checking me out, I can understand that. The hangar manager in Beijing is a friend of mine from school, he can get me a flying job for five hundred dollars.

Shui Ta   That's a lot of money.

Yang Sun   That's 'cause he has to find a pilot guilty of negligence and the pilot he's thinking of has a large family, so he's extremely conscientious and professional. D'you see? This is between you and me, by the way – Shen Te doesn't need to know about it.

Shui Ta   But couldn't this hangar manager find *you* guilty of something a month from now?

Yang Sun   Uh-uh. Not me. No negligence with me. I've been out of a job long enough.

Shui Ta (*nods*)   The hungry horse pulls the cart home quicker. (*Studies him for a moment.*) You're asking a lot of my cousin, Mr Yang Sun. Give up her shop, leave her home and her friends behind and put herself completely in your hands. I assume you're planning to marry her?

Yang Sun   I'd be prepared to do that.

Shui Ta   Then isn't it foolish to sell off the shop? A quick sale won't fetch much. Why not work in the shop yourself?

Yang Sun   Me, a pilot, working behind a counter? 'What kind of cigar are you looking for, sir?' That's no career for Yang Sun.

Shui Ta   So, how much does a pilot make?

Yang Sun (*pulls a letter from his bag*)   I'll be paid one hundred and fifty silver dollars a month! Look. And look at the stamp. Beijing.

Shui Ta   It's a fair sum.

Yang Sun   You think I fly for free?

Shui Ta   My cousin's asked me to help you get this job, Mr Yang Sun, which obviously means everything to you. And I think she should be allowed to follow her heart and discover the joys of love, etc. So, yes, I will consent to the sale of her shop. There's Mrs Mi Tsu now, the tobacco merchant.

Mi Tsu   Good day, Mr Shui Ta. Is it true you're selling the shop?

Shui Ta   My cousin's getting married and her future husband, Mr Yang Sun here, is taking her to Beijing to start a new life. If I can get enough for the tobacco, I'll sell.

Mi Tsu   How much are you asking?

Yang Sun   Five hundred straight up.

Mi Tsu   What did it cost you?

Shui Ta   My cousin paid a thousand for it, and hardly any of it's been sold.

Mi Tsu   A thousand? Then she was ripped off. Move out the day after tomorrow, I'll give you three hundred for the whole shop.

Yang Sun   It's not enough. (*Like an auctioneer.*) First-class tobacco, only recently acquired, in excellent condition, factory price: a thousand dollars. In addition, all shop furnishings plus a week-on-week growing customer base all for the unique price of only five hundred dollars . . . ! Snap it up quick. You're an intelligent woman, you know about life. (*Stroking her.*) You know love too, I'm sure. Love, it makes you gaga – it makes you shout who the hell cares about profit or common sense! And what an opportunity love's created for an astute businesswoman . . .

Mi Tsu (*not immune to this, but remaining firm*)   Three hundred dollars.

Yang Sun (*takes* **Shui Ta** *to one side*)   OK, it's not enough but three hundred in cash is a good start.

Shui Ta (*alarmed*)   But you won't get the job for three hundred.

Yang Sun   But what else would I do with the shop?

Shui Ta   But then everything's gone – what will you live on?

Yang Sun   I'll have three hundred dollars. (*To* **Mi Tsu.**) It's a deal. Three hundred for the whole lot. When do we get the money?

Mi Tsu   Right now. (*Pulls out the money.*) Three hundred dollars. My contribution towards young love.

Yang Sun (*to* **Shui Ta**)   Write three hundred on the contract. I see Shen Te's already signed it.

Shui Ta *writes on the contract, hands it to* **Mi Tsu.** **Yang Sun** *takes the money.*

Mi Tsu   Good day to you both. My regards to Miss Shen Te.

She exits.

Yang Sun (*sits down, exhausted*)   There we go. Job done.

Shui Ta   But it's not enough.

Yang Sun   I know. We're two hundred short. It's all right, you'll get it from somewhere.

Shui Ta   How, without stealing?

Yang Sun   Your cousin told me you're a man who knows about money.

Shui Ta   Maybe I am. (*Slowly.*) I suppose it is Shen Te's happiness we're dealing with here. It's said that a person must be kind to themselves but sympathise with themselves also.

Yang Sun   So you'll see to it. Oh, man, I'm going to fly again!

Shui Ta (*bows, smiling*)   A pilot must fly. (*Casually.*) Do you have any money of your own? For the journey to Beijing?

Yang Sun   Course I have.

Shui Ta   How much?

Yang Sun   I'll get it, even if it means stealing it.

Shui Ta   I see. So that's more money that has to be found.

Yang Sun   All right, calm down. I'll get to Beijing, don't you worry.

Shui Ta   Two tickets won't be cheap.

Yang Sun   No, I'm leaving the girl here. I don't want her being a burden to me, not while I'm settling in.

Shui Ta   I see.

Yang Sun   Don't look at me like that. I've got to grab this chance.

Shui Ta   And what's my cousin going to live off?

Yang Sun   Nothing you can do for her?

Shui Ta   I can try. (*Pause.*) Give me the three hundred, for safe keeping. You'll get it back when you can show me two tickets to Beijing.

Yang Sun   You don't trust me?

Shui Ta   I don't trust anybody.

Yang Sun   Same here. (*They stare at each other.*) If you want to interfere with the course of true love, on you go. I can see we're not going to agree here. I'll ask Shen Te for the rest of the cash.

Shui Ta   You really believe she'll sacrifice everything for you? Even when she finds out you're not even taking her with you?

Yang Sun   Yes, she will. Even then.

Shui Ta   And my opposition to this doesn't bother you?

Yang Sun   Not really, no.

Shui Ta   Or that Shen Te's an intelligent, rational human being?

Yang Sun (*amused*)   You think she'll want to listen to your advice? You're forgetting the power of love and the desires of the flesh. You want her to be rational? It's not going to happen. The poor girl's been neglected her whole life. I only have to put my hand gently on her shoulder and whisper, 'Come with me,' and she'll hear bells ringing and be happy to sell her own mother.

Shui Ta (*pained*)   Mr Yang Sun . . . !

Yang Sun   Mr . . . whateveryou'recalled!

Shui Ta   My cousin's devoted to you because . . .

Yang Sun   Because it's *my* hands she wants stroking her tits. So stick that in one of your pipes and smoke it.

He takes another cigar, puts a few more in his pocket, finally grabs the whole box and sticks it under his arm.

I'm going outside to wait for her. And if she gets home late it's 'cause I took her out for something to eat to talk intimately to each other about two hundred dollars.

He exits.

Mrs Shin (*sticks her head out from the back*)   What a charmer he is.

Shui Ta (*screams*)   The shop's ruined! He's not in love with her! I'm lost!

He begins to walk around like a captive animal, repeating again and again 'The shop's ruined', until he suddenly stops and addresses **Mrs Shin**.

Shui Ta   You grew up in the gutter, Mrs Shin, and so did I. Are we irresponsible? No. Do we have the necessary brutality? Yes. I'd happily grab you by the neck and shake you until you spit out the cash you stole from me. You know I would. The times are awful and this city's hell, but we still go on pulling ourselves up the slippery slope. Then disaster – a girl falls in love and that's it, she's lost. One sign of weakness and it's all over with. How do you not show weakness? How do you guard against love, the most deadly weakness of all? Love's impossible; it asks everything of you. But how can a person live always watching their back? What kind of world is that?

> Sweet caresses become silent throttling.
> The sigh of love becomes a cry of fear.
> Why are those vultures circling overhead?
> They see a girl going out on a date.

Go and get the barber, Mr Shu Fu, immediately!

Mrs Shin *goes out.*

Shui Ta *paces around again until* **Shu Fu** *walks in, followed by* **Mrs Shin**, *who then withdraws at a wave from* **Shu Fu**.

Shui Ta   I gather, sir, you've recently expressed some interest in my cousin. I'm putting aside all the rules of decency and modesty because the young lady finds herself at this moment in the greatest danger.

Shu Fu   Oh.

Shui Ta   A shop-owner less than an hour ago, she's now little more than a vagrant. Mr Shu Fu, this shop is ruined.

Shu Fu   Mr. Shui Ta, the shop is a loss, true, but remember there is goodness in Miss Shen Te's heart. That is her charm. It is why she's known throughout the district as the Angel of the Suburbs.

Shui Ta   Her goodness has cost her her business! We must put a stop to it.

Shu Fu   May I suggest another way? Put aside what's happened. Let Shen Te continue as she is. It's in her nature. I hear she feeds four people every morning – but what if she was able to feed four hundred? I know she's also looking to shelter some of our homeless – well then, I have a few houses behind my cattle shed, she can use them. It's what she's good at, this kind of thing, isn't it? So leave her to it. It's what she would want, I'm sure.

Shui Ta   And I'm sure she'll have nothing but admiration for you, Mr Shu Fu.

Shu Fu   Would you agree to her and I having dinner soon? In an intimate but highly reputable restaurant.

Shui Ta   I'll let her know immediately. She will listen to common sense this time. She's very upset about her shop, which she likes to think was a gift from the Gods. If you'd kindly wait for a minute or so.

He goes into the back of the shop.

Mrs Shin (*puts her head through the door*)   Are congratulations in order?

Shu Fu   I'd say so. Tell Miss Shen Te's guests that from tonight they're sleeping in the houses behind my cattle shed.

She grins and nods. **Shu Fu** *addresses the audience.*

Shu Fu   What do you think of me, ladies and gentlemen? Could such an esteemed man do more? Be more unselfish? More understanding? More forward-looking? An intimate dinner may sound vulgar to you but don't worry, nothing will happen. No physical contact at all, not even an apparently accidental brush of hands when passing the salt. It will be a meeting of minds. Two people who can help each other. I should make sure there's a vase of flowers on the table. White chrysanthemums. (*He makes a note.*) No, there'll be no exploiting or taking advantage of her situation – I will humbly and sincerely offer my assistance. And guidance. Which I believe Miss Shen Te will acknowledge with a grateful glance. Perhaps more than grateful.

Mrs Shin Did everything turn out as you wanted, Mr. Shu Fu?

Shu Fu Exactly as I wanted. There are going to be changes around here, effective immediately. A certain individual will be sent packing. And this shop will be bought back and will start trading again. And let it be known that in future no one is to question or prey upon the reputation of Szechuan's most virtuous young lady. So, what do we know about this Yang Sun?

Shu Fu Not much except that he's the dirtiest, most lazy –

Shu Fu He's nothing. He doesn't exist. He is history, Mrs Shin.

Enter **Yang Sun**.

Yang Sun What's going on here?

Mrs Shin Mr Shu Fu, d'you want me to call Mr Shui Ta? He wouldn't want strangers loitering in his shop.

Shu Fu Miss Shen Te has an important meeting with Mr Shui Ta which can't be interrupted.

Yang Sun What, she's here? I didn't see her coming in. What meeting? I should have been told about this.

Shu Fu *prevents him from going into the back room.*

Shu Fu I know who you are, sir. And you should know that Miss Shen Te and I are about to announce our engagement.

Yang Sun What?

Mrs Shin   Didn't see that coming, did you?

Yang Sun *struggles with* **Shu Fu** *to get into the back room.* **Shen Te** *steps out.*

Shu Fu   I'm sorry, my dear. Perhaps you can explain to –

Yang Sun   What's going on here? Have you gone mad?

Shen Te (*breathless*)   Yang Sun, my cousin and Mr Shu Fu have come to an agreement that I take some time to consider Mr Shu Fu's ideas about how to help the unfortunate people of this neighbourhood. (*Pause.*) Also, my cousin is absolutely dead set against our relationship.

Yang Sun   And you agree with him?

Shen Te   Yes.

Pause.

Yang Sun   Did they tell you I'm a bad person?

Shen Te *remains silent.*

Yang Sun   And maybe they're right, maybe I am. But that's the reason I need you. I'm a humble man. No capital, not many manners. But I have to stand up for myself. Look at me. You really think I wouldn't love you if you had no money? They're forcing you to do something that'll make you unhappy. (*He moves to her. Quietly.*) Look at him. Have you no eyes in your head? You poor thing, what're they trying to do to you now? Force you into marriage? If I hadn't come along, they'd have had you hanging up in the slaughterhouse by now. Tell me straight, if it hadn't been for me, would you have gone off with him?

Shen Te   Yes.

Yang Sun   A man you don't love.

Shen Te   Yes.

Yang Sun   Have you forgotten everything? The rain?

Shen Te   No.

Yang Sun   How you cut me down from the branch, bought me a cup of water, promised me the money so I could fly again . . . ?

Shen Te (*shaking*)   What do you want?

Yang Sun   Come away with me.

Shen Te   Mr Shu Fu, forgive me, I want to go with Yang Sun.

Yang Sun   Get your shawl, the blue shawl you wore.

Shen Te *fetches the shawl, which she was wearing in the park.*

Yang Sun   We're lovers, just so you know.

He takes her to the door.

Where did you put the key to the shop?

He takes it out of her pocket and gives it to **Mrs Shin**.

Yang Sun   Leave it on the doorstep when you've finished here. Let's go, Shen Te.

Shu Fu   This is rape! (*Calls into the back.*) Mr Shui Ta!

Yang Sun   Don't shout like that in here.

Shen Te   Please don't call my cousin, Mr Shu Fu. I know he doesn't agree with me but he's wrong, I can feel it now, he's wrong.

(*To the audience.*)
    I want to go with the man I love.
    I don't want to have to calculate what it'll cost.
    I don't want to consider whether it's good.
    I only want to go with the man I love.

Yang Sun   And that's me.

They exit together.

Interlude

Outside a tea shop.

Shen Te *carries a small sack under her arm.*

Shen Te   I've never seen the city so early in the morning.
At this hour I usually lie with the blanket pulled over my head,
afraid to face the day. But this morning I walked among the
paper boys and the men who sprinkle the asphalt roads with
water and the ox carts loaded with fresh vegetables from the
countryside.

I always heard that when you're in love you walk on clouds,
but the real beauty is that you walk on earth. The houses are
like heaps of rubble with lights burning in them and the sky
is pink but still clear because there's no dust. I tell you, when
you're not in love you miss out on so much – you don't get to
see the city as it rises in the morning like a dedicated old
labourer breathing in the fresh air as he reaches for his work
tools.

And here's the House of Bliss, the tea house where I have to
sell this sack so that Yang Sun can fly again.

*She's about to go in, when some people come out. They're addicts, freezing,
unsteady on their feet. A young man pulls out his wallet, finds it empty,
throws it away. A woman vomits. An ugly old man holds up a very young
and very doped girl.*

This is terrible. Heroin has destroyed them. (*Looks at her sack,
shocked.*) This is poison. How could I think of selling it? It's not
even mine. What was I thinking of? I let my emotions rule me
and threw myself back into Yang Sun's arms again. I couldn't
resist his voice and his caresses. The awful things he said to
Shui Ta had no effect on Shen Te. When he put his arms
around me, all I thought was: the Gods wanted me to be good
to myself.

> Not let anyone go to ruin,
> Not even oneself.

To bring happiness to everyone,
Including oneself,
That is good.

He's like a hurricane heading for Beijing who just blew away my shop. But he's not a bad man and he loves me. As long as I'm with him, he won't do anything bad. What one man says to other men doesn't mean a thing. He wants to look big and strong and tough. When I tell him what I saw here, he'll understand. He'd rather go and work with me at the cement factory than be a pilot on the back of others' misery. Will I be strong enough to summon up the good in him? Now, about to marry him, I'm caught between fear and joy.

Six

A private room in a cheap restaurant in the suburbs.

*A **Waiter** pours wine for the wedding guests. Next to **Shen Te** stand the **Grandfather**, the **Sister-in-Law**, the **Niece**, **Mrs Shin** and the **Unemployed Man**. A **Priest** stands in the corner alone. At the front, **Yang Sun**, wearing a dinner jacket, speaks with his mother, **Mrs Yang**.*

Yang Sun Bad news, Mother. She's just told me she can't raise the extra two hundred dollars.

Mrs Yang What did you say? Because if she can't, you can't marry her.

Yang Sun I told her I wanted to talk to her cousin. She's so pig-headed.

Mrs Yang But he wants to marry her off to the barber.

Yang Sun It's been dealt with. The barber's out the picture. Shui Ta will see sense – the shop's sold now and if I don't get the rest of the money, I'll have no job either.

Mrs Yang I'll stand outside and watch for him. You go to your bride.

Shen Te (*to the audience as she pours wine*)   I wasn't wrong about him. He took the disappointment well. Not being able to fly again must have hit him hard, but look at him now, he's smiling and joking. I love him with all my heart.

She waves **Yang Sun** *over.*

Shen Te   We haven't made a toast yet.

Yang Sun   What shall we toast to?

Shen Te   The future.

They drink.

Yang Sun   To a time when the bridegroom won't have to rent his dinner jacket.

Shen Te   And the bride's dress gets caught in the rain occasionally.

Yang Sun   That what we wish for we get.

Shen Te   And that it comes to us soon.

Mrs Yang *goes to leave, talking to* **Mrs Shin**.

Mrs Yang   I'm so happy for my son. I always told him he could get any girl he wanted. He's a fully qualified mechanic and pilot. And do you know what he told me a moment ago? That he's marrying for love. Money isn't everything. It's true love, I tell you. (*To the* **Sister-in-Law**.) It had to happen sometime. It's so difficult for a mother to let them go, so difficult. (*Calls over to the* **Priest**.) Don't make the ceremony too short, you hear? If you take as much time over it as you took negotiating your fee, that'll be fine. (*To* **Shen Te**.) Just a tiny delay, my dear. We're still waiting on one of the guests. (*To everyone.*) Excuse me please.

She exits.

Sister-in-Law   As long as there's wine, we're happy to wait.

They sit down.

Unemployed Man   We're not missing anything.

Yang Sun (*loudly, jokily*)   Shen Te, my love, since our wedding happened at such short notice, I think we should have a quick test before we exchange vows. (*To the guests.*) Who knows what kind of wife I'm getting? First question: can she make five cups of tea from three tea leaves?

Shen Te   No.

Yang Sun   So I won't be drinking much tea then. Are you able to sleep on a straw mat the size of the priest's prayer book?

Shen Te   With you?

Yang Sun   On your own.

Shen Te   Then, no, I can't.

Yang Sun   I'm shocked, what kind of woman is this, soon to be my wife?

Everyone laughs. **Mrs Yang** *enters behind* **Shen Te**. *Shrugging her shoulders, she indicates to* **Yang Sun** *that no one's arrived. The* **Priest** *points to his watch.*

Mrs Yang   Hold your horses. A few more minutes. Everyone's enjoying themselves.

She sits down with the guests.

Shen Te   How are we going to pay for this?

Mrs Yang   Let's not talk business today. Brings such a vulgar tone to the happy occasion, d'you not think?

The doorbell rings. Everyone looks towards the door. No one enters.

Shen Te   Who's your mother waiting for, Yang Sun?

Yang Sun   It's a surprise. By the way, how's your cousin, Shui Ta? I liked him. Sensible head on his shoulders. What's wrong with you?

Shen Te   I don't know. I don't want to think about him.

Yang Sun   Why not?

Shen Te   Because if you like him, you can't love me.

Yang Sun   Then I hope the Three Devils have him: the Marsh Devil, the Fog Devil and the Gas-Shortage Devil. Drink, pig-headed girl.

He forces her to drink.

Sister-in-Law (*to* **Mrs Shin**)   Something fishy's going on here.

Mrs Shin   Did you expect anything else?

*The **Priest** walks resolutely over to **Mrs Yang**, holding up his watch.*

Priest   I have to go, Mrs Yang. I have another wedding and a funeral first thing in the morning.

Mrs Yang   D'you think I want the delay? We were hoping we'd only need the one jug of wine. See how low it's getting. (*Loudly to* **Shen Te**.) Dear Shen Te, I can't understand why your cousin's making us wait like this.

Shen Te   My cousin?

Mrs Yang   It's him we're all waiting for. Is it so old-fashioned to believe that the bride's close relatives should be present on her wedding day?

Shen Te   Oh, Yang Sun, is this because of the extra two hundred dollars?

Yang Sun (*not looking at her*)   She's just told you why – she's old-fashioned. I respect that. We'll wait for fifteen minutes and if he's not here by then we'll go ahead.

Mrs Yang   I assume you've all heard that my son is about to start work as a mail pilot. I'm delighted. A good income's essential in times like these.

Sister-in-Law   The job's in Beijing, isn't it?

Mrs Yang   Yes, Beijing.

Shen Te   Yang Sun, why haven't you told her you're not going to Beijing?

Yang Sun   Your cousin can if he thinks the same way. I've changed my mind. I want to go.

Shen Te (*shocked*)   Yang Sun!

Yang Sun   I hate Szechuan! I hate this city! When I half close my eyes, d'you know how I see them all? As horses. Turning their heads up to the sky, petrified. What's that thundering over their heads? Are they still useful? Are they to be boiled down into glue? They can all bite each other to death in their horse town. I just want out of here.

Shen Te   But I've told you, I can't raise the two hundred.

Yang Sun   I know, you've told me. That's why I want to see your cousin. Go and have a drink and leave the business affairs to us.

Shen Te   But my cousin can't come!

Yang Sun   What d'you mean?

Shen Te   He's not around any more.

Yang Sun   So we've no future then, have we?

Shen Te   We still have three hundred dollars. We could buy back some of our tobacco and sell it outside the cement factory.

Yang Sun   You think I'd stand on the street and sell tobacco to cement workers? Forget it. I'd rather blow all the money in one night – or just throw it in the river. Your cousin's coming – and he'll have the money with him.

Shen Te   He can't come!

Yang Sun   I thought he couldn't stay away.

Shen Te   He can't be where I am.

Yang Sun   Very cryptic . . .

Shen Te   You have to understand . . . it's *me* that loves you. Shui Ta loves nobody. He wanted you to have the three hundred because of the pilot's job but he won't bring the rest.

Yang Sun   Why not?

Shen Te (*looks into his eyes*)   He told me you only bought one ticket to Beijing.

Yang Sun   I did – yesterday – but look what I have today.

Pulls two pieces of paper halfway out his pocket.

Careful, in case my mother sees. Two tickets to Beijing, one for me, one for you. So d'you think your cousin will still be against the marriage?

Shen Te   No. It's a good job. And I don't have the shop any more . . .

Yang Sun   *You* were the reason I sold all the furniture.

Shen Te   Don't say any more. Don't show me the tickets. I'm scared I'll leave with you right now. But, Yang Sun, I don't have the two hundred dollars you want.

Yang Sun   So what'm I going to do? (*Pause.*) Have a drink! Or are you one of those timid wet-blanket types? 'Cause I don't want a wife like that. When I drink, I dream I'll fly again. And when you drink, maybe, just maybe, you'll understand me.

Shen Te   I do understand you. But I can't help you.

Yang Sun   'Here's an aeroplane for you, darling, but I'm afraid it's only got the one wing.'

Shen Te   It would be dishonest to take that job in Beijing. I need the three hundred dollars back. Give it back.

Yang Sun   'Give it back.' What're you talking about? D'you want to be my wife or not? 'Cause you're betraying me, y'know that? Thank God it's not up to you any more, it's all been agreed.

Mrs Yang (*coldly*)   Yang Sun, are you sure this cousin's coming? He's not staying away for some reason you're not telling me?

Yang Sun   What're you on about, Mother? We're best mates. Open the door wider so he'll see us when he walks down the street.

*He goes to the door, kicks it open. Comes back, swaying slightly from the drink, sits down next to **Shen Te**.*

Yang Sun   We'll keep waiting. Your cousin's got more sense than you. Like he said, love's a part of life. And he knows what that'd mean to you: no shop any more and no wedding either.

They wait.

Mrs Yang   Listen.

They hear footsteps. Everyone looks towards the door but the footsteps move past and fade away.

Mrs Shin   This is going to be a disaster. I can feel it, I can smell it. The bride wants a wedding but the groom's only interested in her cousin.

Yang Sun   Taking his bloody time, isn't he?

Shen Te (*quietly*)   Yang Sun . . .

Yang Sun   I have to sit here with two tickets in my pocket next to a dunce who can't add up. Won't be long before you send the police after me to get your money back.

Shen Te (*to the audience*)   He's a bad man – and he wants me to be bad too. I'm in love with him and all he cares about is Shui Ta. And all around us sit the vulnerable and the poor who'll be waiting for rice outside my door tomorrow morning. And in Beijing a pilot I've never met is worried sick about his job. It's them, my faith in them that keeps me going.

Yang Sun (*stares at the almost empty wine jug*)   This wine jug will be our clock. We're poor people, so when it's all drunk, time's up.

Mrs Yang *signals for him to be quiet. She's heard more footsteps.*

Waiter   Another jug of wine, Mrs Yang?

Mrs Yang   I think we've had enough. Wine makes you so hot, doesn't it?

Mrs Shin   Costs a bit too.

Mrs Yang   I always sweat when I drink.

Waiter   I must ask you to settle up then.

Mrs Yang (*ignoring him*)   Ladies and gentlemen, a little more patience, please, the cousin is on his way. (*To the* **Waiter**.) Don't annoy us, we're celebrating.

Waiter   I'm serving nothing else until the bill's paid.

Mrs Yang   But everyone knows me around here.

Waiter   Exactly.

Mrs Yang   The service here is appalling. Don't you agree, Yang Sun?

Priest   I have to go.

He exits importantly.

Mrs Yang (*desperately*)   No one leave their seats. The priest'll be back in a few minutes.

Yang Sun   Forget it, Mother. Ladies and gentlemen, seeing as the priest has left, there's no need to stay a moment longer.

Sister-in-Law   C'mon, Grandad.

Grandfather (*solemnly empties his glass*)   To the bride.

Niece (*to* **Shen Te**)   Don't mind him. He means well. He's fond of you.

Mrs Shin   I said it, didn't I? A disaster.

All the guests leave.

Shen Te (*to* **Yang Sun**)   Do you want me to leave too?

Yang Sun   No, you wait.

He pulls at her wedding clothes, skewing them.

Yang Sun   It's your wedding day, isn't it? I'm still waiting and the old lady's still waiting too. She wants to see her hawk soaring in the sky – but pigs will fly before that ever happens. (*To the empty chairs as if the guests were still there.*) Ladies and gentlemen, what's happened to you? D'you not like it here? The wedding's only been delayed a little while because of the important cousin's no-show and because the bride doesn't know what love is. So, for you all, while you wait, I, the groom will sing you a song.

He sings 'The Song of St Nevercome's Day'.

As you lay in your wretched cradle
This story you'll have heard as a baby
A poor woman's son will inherit the throne
Pigs will fly, pigs will fly
When a poor woman's son will inherit the throne.

And on that day goodness will be rewarded
And crime will never pay
And Labour and Wages will respect each other
And bread and salt will be free
Pigs will fly, pigs will fly
Bread and salt will be free.

And grass will grow green in the sky
And rivers run upstream
And Man will be good and watch in wonder
As the earth turns to paradise
Pigs will fly, pigs will fly
When the earth turns to paradise.

And on that day I'll be a pilot
And you'll become a general
And you, poor woman, will have a day off
And you'll get a job that pays well
Pigs will fly, pigs will fly
You'll get a job that pays well.

And boy are we tired of waiting
For this new age to be born

We get told it won't wait until nightfall
No, this will all happen at dawn.
Pigs will fly, pigs will fly
All this will happen at dawn.

And grass will grow green in the sky
And rivers run upstream
And Man will wake in a paradise
The answer to all of his dreams
Pigs will fly, pigs will fly
The answer to all of his dreams.

Mrs Yang   He's not coming.

The three of them sit down. Two of them look towards the door.

Interlude

Wang's *sleeping place.*

Wang *sees the* **Gods** *in his dreams. He has fallen asleep over a large book.*

Wang   I'm so glad you've come, Divinities. Something's been troubling me. It's from this book I found in the ruined hut of a priest who moved away to become an unskilled labourer in the cement factory. Can I read it to you?

With his left hand, he turns the pages of an imaginary book in his lap, then lifting it up, leaving the real book where it is.

'In Sung there is a place known as Thornwood where catalpa, cypress and mulberry trees grow. Those trees which measure nine or ten inches in circumference are cut down by people who want bars for their dog kennels. The trees with a circumference of three or four feet are cut down by the rich and distinguished families who want them as planks for their coffins. And the trees with a circumference of seven or eight feet are cut down by people wanting roof-beams for their luxurious villas. And so it is that none of the trees in Thornwood reach the end of their life cycle and instead are cut down prematurely by the axe and the saw. Such is the curse of usefulness.'

Third God   But that means that the most useless would be the best.

Wang   No, not the best, the most fortunate.

First God   The things people write!

Second God   Why are you so taken with this parable, water seller?

Wang   Because of Shen Te. She's failed in love because she was so kind to others. Maybe she really is too good for this world.

First God   Nonsense, you weak, unhappy man. You're letting doubt and lice eat away at you.

Wang   Forgive me. I only thought perhaps you might be able to intervene.

First God   Impossible.

He points to the **Third God***, who has a black eye from a fight.*

First God   Only yesterday, this one here intervened in a dispute. You can see what happened to him.

Wang   But her cousin's had to come back again – and he's a very clever and able man, but even he could do nothing. It looks like the shop's lost.

Third God (*alarmed*)   Perhaps we should help.

First God   No, she has to help herself.

Second God (*firmly*)   The worse the situation, the better the person that emerges. Suffering purifies.

First God   We've put all our hopes in her.

Third God   Our search has not gone well. We've witnessed some attempts to be good here and there, some steady resolve, noble principles, but they alone don't make a good person. Whenever we do meet someone halfway good, they're living in the most inhumane circumstances. (*Confidentially.*) And trying to find a room for the night . . . Guess where we've been sleeping. The straw's a clue.

Wang   But couldn't you at least –

Gods   No. We are only observers. Shen Te will find her way on this dark earth. Her strength will grow as her burden increases. Be patient, water seller, everything will turn out . . .

*The **Gods** have steadily become paler, their voices fainter. Now they disappear.*

Seven

*A yard behind **Shen Te**'s tobacco shop.*

*Household goods on a cart. **Shen Te** and **Mrs Shin** take washing off the line.*

Mrs Shin   So, not only have you lost your shop but the whole neighbourhood knows your pilot's been drinking the money away in dodgy dives all over town.

Shen Te *stays silent.*

Mrs Shin   You've lost everything – husband, tobacco, your home. That's what you get trying to be a cut above the rest of us. What will you live off now?

Shen Te   Maybe I can earn some money sorting tobacco.

*A **Child** appears in the entrance to the yard.*

Mrs Shin (*shoos him away*)   Get away! (*To **Shen Te**.*) One whiff of ruin and the street rats come scuttling.

Shen Te   Let him rummage through the junk. He might find something he can use.

Mrs Shin   If there's anything useful, I'll have it. You haven't paid me for the laundry yet. Get out, or I'll call the police!

The **Child** *goes.*

Shen Te   Why are you so mean?

(*To the audience.*)
    Is it not exhausting
    To kick out at a fellow human being?
    The veins on your forehead
    Swell up from the effort it takes to be greedy.
    A hand, reaching out,
    Can give and take with equal ease.
    Only when it grabs, does it need effort.
    Oh, the temptation to give!
    How gratifying it is to be kind!
    A good word escapes like a sigh of pleasure.

Mrs Shin   Don't let your cousin hear you talking like that. What are his trousers doing here? Did he leave naked?

Shen Te   He's got two pairs.

Mrs Shin   I thought you said he'd gone for good. How could he forget a pair of trousers?

Shen Te   Maybe he doesn't need them any more.

Mrs Shin   You can take them with you then.

Shen Te   No.

The **Carpenter** *appears in the entrance to the yard.*

Carpenter   Good day, Miss Shen Te. People are saying the barber Shu Fu is housing the homeless. Is it true?

Mrs Shin   It was. But then someone turned him down so the houses are gone.

Carpenter   I've nowhere to take my family.

Mrs Shin (*about* **Shen Te**)   It won't be long before she'll be asking *you* for shelter.

The **Carpenter** *exits, abjectly.*

Mrs Shin   There's plenty more like him around.

Shen Te   This is awful.

Mrs Shin (*about the* **Carpenter**)   There's always the fishing huts by the river for them. You're still besotted by that pilot even after the way he treated you. Don't you care he's a bad man?

Shen Te   It all comes from poverty.

(*To the audience.*)
    I saw his cheeks puff out in the night
    While he was sleeping: he looked evil.
    And in the morning I held his jacket up to the light
    And I could see the wall through it.
    Then when I saw his deceiving smile I was disgusted
    But when I saw the holes in his shoes, I fell in love again.

Mrs Shin   So now you're defending him? (*Angrily.*) I wish you'd bloody well piss off.

Shen Te (*sways while she takes the washing off the line*)   I feel a bit dizzy.

Mrs Shin (*takes the washing from her*)   Maybe he's left a baby inside you as well . . . (*Laughs.*) That pilot's had you every which way.

She exits carrying basket.

Shen Te (*quietly*)   Oh joy! A little person growing in my body. No one can tell yet, but he's there. The world's secretly expecting him. In the cities they're already whispering: 'Here comes someone we'll have to reckon with.'

She presents her little son to the audience.

    A pilot!
    Greet the new conqueror
    Of uncharted regions and inaccessible mountains.
    Who carries over endless deserts
    The mail from one person to another.

She starts to walk up and down, taking her little son by the hand.

C'mon, son, take a look at the world. Here, this is a tree. Bow
to it and say hello. (*Shows him how to bow.*) So now you know
each other. Hold on, here comes the water seller. He's a friend,
don't be afraid, shake his hand. 'A cup of fresh water for my
son, please. It's hot.' (*She gives him the cup.*) Oh, the policeman.
Him, we avoid. Maybe we'll pick some cherries from the
garden of rich Mr Feh Pung. We can't let him see us. You want
cherries, don't you? Careful, son.

They walk cautiously, looking around.

No, you can't walk straight over and help yourself.

He appears to be pulling her away, but she resists.

We have to be careful. (*She gives in.*) All right, if you want to
walk straight up to them . . . (*She lifts him up.*) Can you reach
the cherries? Put them in your mouth, it's a good place to keep
them. (*She eats one.*) It tastes lovely. Damn, the policeman! Now
we have to run.

They run away.

There's the road. Calm now, walk slowly, so that we won't be
noticed. As if nothing had happened . . .

She sings as she walks with her son.

> A plum, for no reason at all,
> Attacked a tramp as he hobbled about
> But the fellow was quick,
> Smashed the plum with a stick,
> And the plum ended up in his mouth.

The **Child** *has reappeared in the entrance to the yard. He looks at*
Shen Te*'s performance in astonishment. Suddenly she notices him and
beckons him into the yard.*

Child   Where are you going?

Shen Te   I don't know, Mi Tsu.

The **Child** *rubs his tummy and looks at* **Shen Te** *expectantly.*

Shen Te   No rice left, not a single grain.

Child   Stay.

Shen Te   I'd like to.

We can hear the cry of the water seller: 'Water for sale!'

Child   I'm thirsty.

Shen Te   That I can fix for you. C'mon, little man. (*To the audience.*) Did you all hear that? There's a child here from tomorrow who's asking for water today. (*To the child.*) Hang on a moment.

She runs to the entrance of the yard, where **Wang** *has appeared.*

Wang   Hello, Shen Te. I'm sorry about your shop.

Shen Te   That doesn't matter. I've just experienced incredible joy. I'm having a child, Wang. I'm glad you're here, I was bursting to tell someone. But don't tell anyone else, I don't want Yang Sun finding out. I'll take a cup of water.

He gives her a cup of water. When she turns round, she stops in her tracks, seeing the **Child** *rummaging in the bin. He pulls something out and eats it.*

Shen Te (*to* **Wang**)   Go now. I don't feel very well.

She pushes him away.

He's hungry. He's going through the rubbish bin.

She picks up the **Child** *and, while she talks, shows the audience his small grey mouth. The music for 'The Song of the Powerlessness of the Gods and the Good' starts as she speaks.*

Shen Te
  Oh my son, my little pilot,
  What kind of world will you be born into?
  They'll want you scavenging through rubbish bins, you too.

  Look at his little grey mouth!
  Is that how you treat your fellow creatures?
  Have you no pity for the fruit of your own womb?
  No compassion for yourselves, you unhappy people.
  Well, at least, I'll protect my own

Even if I have to become a tigress.
From today onwards, now that I've seen this
I'll cut myself off from everyone
And not rest until I've saved my son.
What I've learnt in the school of the gutter,
The senseless violence and wicked deceit,
Is all for you.
I shall be good to you, my son,
And to everyone else be a tigress,
A wild animal, if I must.
And I must.

Interlude

Wang *walks along the curtain as if it were a road. He stops and addresses the audience.*

Wang   Can you tell me, good people, where Miss Shen Te from Sandalmakers Lane has gone? She disappeared five months ago and she hasn't been seen since. Her cousin appeared suddenly – for the third time – and since then some strange business has been going on in the tobacco shop. A profitable business, yes, but dishonourable. Evil. (*Quietly.*) Heroin. The worst of it is, I can't contact the Gods any more. Perhaps it's the worry keeping me awake at night so I don't dream any more. If you see Shen Te, tell her to get in touch. We miss her round here – the good people are always missed.

He walks away.

Eight

Shen Te's *tobacco shop.*

The shop has become an office with armchairs and beautiful carpets.
Shui Ta, *well dressed and fat, is seeing out the* **Wife**, **Husband** *and* **Nephew** *who visited* **Shen Te** *on the day she opened her shop.* **Mrs**

Shin, *dressed in flashy new clothes, watches him, amused. Outside, it's raining.*

Shui Ta   For the tenth time. I never saw any sacks in the back room!

Wife   In that case we'll write to Miss Shen Te. What's her address?

Shui Ta   No idea, sorry.

Nephew   The sacks are gone, but you got wealthy . . .

Shui Ta   So it would appear.

Mrs Shin   I'd let the matter drop. After all, Mr Shui Ta has employed most of your family in his tobacco factory. His patience is wearing thin.

Wife   But the work's ruining the boy's health.

Shui Ta *and* **Mrs Shin** *remain silent.*

Husband   Let's go. We've no proof about the sacks. Maybe Shen Te will return some day.

Shui Ta *shrugs. The* **Wife**, **Husband** *and* **Nephew** *leave angrily.*

Shui Ta (*weakly*)   Work ruining his health? Work's work.

Mrs Shin   They'd have had no idea what to do with those sacks. It needed know-how to make real money from it. That's what you did.

Shui Ta (*sitting down*)   I'm dizzy again.

Mrs Shin   'Cause you're seven months gone, that's why. The excitement's bad for you. You're lucky you've got me to help you. (*She laughs.*)

Shui Ta (*weakly*)   Can I count on you, Mrs Shin?

Mrs Shin   Absolutely. Course, it'll cost you a bit.

A man wearing fashionable clothes enters. It's the **Unemployed Man** *who was given cigarettes on the opening day of the shop. He's now the* **Agent**.

Agent   Your accounts, Mr Shui Ta. Sales to street clients total fifty dollars. Sales at the House of Bliss . . .

Shui Ta (*with difficulty*)   Go. Tomorrow.

Mrs Shin   Can't you see Mr Shui Ta isn't well?

Agent   There's a problem with the police in the Fourth District. A package fell into the wrong hands.

Mrs Shin   Do something about it then!

The **Agent** *is about to go.*

Shui Ta   Wait. The money!

The **Agent** *hands over the money, leaves.*

Mrs Shin   Open your shirt, you'll be more comfortable.

Shui Ta (*pathetically*)   This is all for the child, Mrs Shin. Only for the child.

Mrs Shin   All for the child.

Shui Ta   I'm putting on so much weight. People must have noticed.

Mrs Shin   They're all saying it's 'cause you're rich.

Shui Ta   What'll become of the little one?

Mrs Shin   Three times a day you ask me this. It'll go into care, the best money can buy.

Shui Ta   Yes. (*Fearfully.*) And he must never see Shui Ta.

Mrs Shin   Never. Always Shen Te.

Shui Ta   But all the neighbourhood gossips . . . And the water seller. They watch the shop like hawks.

Mrs Shin   Drink some water. Why don't you move out of here into a bigger house? Why do I bother? You're still pining for that bloody pilot.

Shui Ta   Rubbish!

A man in ragged clothes appears in the door. It's **Yang Sun**. *He's astonished to see* **Shui Ta** *in the arms of* **Mrs Shin**, *who is helping* **Shui Ta** *to drink the water.*

Yang Sun   Don't want to disturb anything . . .

Shui Ta *gets up with difficulty and stares at him.*

Mrs Shin   Look what we have here.

Yang Sun (*subservient*)   Excuse my clothes, Mr Shui Ta. My luggage got lost somewhere and I didn't want to let the rain stop me from looking up some old friends.

Shui Ta *takes* **Mrs Shin** *to one side before she can say anything.*

Shui Ta   Go and get some clothes.

Mrs Shin   Throw him out. Immediately. I'm warning you.

Shui Ta (*sharply*)   Do what I tell you!

Mrs Shin *exits reluctantly.*

Yang Sun   Woollen rugs – someone's gotten rich. I've heard that everyone calls you the Tobacco King now.

Shui Ta   I got lucky.

Yang Sun   No, you earned it. Some get fat, others stay thin, that's how it is, eh?

Shui Ta   I know you've had your share of bad luck. Are you ill?

Yang Sun   Me? No. Fit as a fiddle.

Shui Ta   That's good to hear. Poor health is a hard thing to be cured of.

Mrs Shin *returns with some clothes from the back room.*

Shui Ta   See if these fit you. The hat might be too big for your head.

Mrs Shin *puts a hat on* **Yang Sun**'s *head.*

Shui Ta   Yes, too big. Get another one, Mrs Shin.

Yang Sun   I don't want a hat. (*Suddenly angry.*) What're you doing? Fobbing me off with an old hat? (*Pulls himself together.*) I need what I came for. (*Servile.*) Mr Shui Ta, why won't you help a man who's fallen on hard times?

Shui Ta   How can I help you?

Mrs Shin   You really don't know? I can tell you what he's wanting . . .

Shui Ta (*beginning to understand*)   No . . . !

Mrs Shin   Heroin.

Shui Ta   Yang Sun!

Yang Sun   Just a small bag. All I need's two or three pipes. I don't care about clothes or food, I just want a pipe.

Shui Ta (*horrified*)   No, not heroin! Don't tell me you're an addict . . . It only brings misery. It's bliss at first, yes, but it quickly turns to misery and suffering.

Yang Sun   I know. I'm already there.

Shui Ta   Stop it, now! You can fight your addiction – you can overcome it, I know you can.

Yang Sun   So speaks Mr Shui Ta, the heroin dealer, who makes his money from the very same misery.

Shui Ta   Water. I'm going to be sick.

Mrs Shin (*fussing about her*)   You've not been well lately, not like you used to be. (*Mockingly.*) Maybe the rain brought Mr Yang Sun. Rain always makes you short-tempered and melancholy, doesn't it . . . ?

Shui Ta   Go, get out of here!

Wang's voice
> I've got water to sell
> I sell water, cups of water
> Now of course it's pissing raining
> Walked for miles to fetch this water

This is how I make my living:
'Come and buy my fresh, pure water!'
But no one wants it
No one pays me
They're too desperate and greedy
       Buy my water, you bastards!

Mrs Shin   There's that water seller again. He's like a broken bloody record!

She exits.

Wang's voice   Are there no good people left in Szechuan? Are there none living here on the square where Shen Te used to live? Where is she? Many months ago, when it was raining, she bought a cup of water from me. Where is she now? Has no one seen her? Heard from her? One night she walked into this house here and never appeared again.

Yang Sun   Give me what I want and I'll shut him up. What the hell's it got to do with him where she is, anyway?

Wang *enters.*

Wang   Mr Shui Ta, I need to ask again: when will Miss Shen Te return? It's six months now since she disappeared.

Shui Ta *remains silent.*

Wang   A lot's happened – most of which wouldn't have if she'd been here.

Shui Ta *is still silent.*

Wang   Rumours are going round that something's happened to her. Her friends are worried sick. D'you have an address for her?

Shui Ta   I'm sorry, Wang, I'm busy right now. Come back next week.

Wang (*agitated*)   People have noticed the rice for the poor is being put out at the door again.

Shui Ta   And what do they have to say about that?

Wang That Shen Te hasn't left town at all.

Shui Ta So, where's she gone?

Wang*'s silent.*

Shui Ta For the last time, Wang, take my advice, if you're Shen Te's friend, stop asking where she is.

Wang The last time I saw her she told me she was pregnant.

Yang Sun What?!

Shui Ta (*quickly*) It was a lie.

Wang You can't shut us up, Mr Shui Ta. A good person isn't easily forgotten. There aren't many of them around.

He exits. **Shui Ta** *stares after him, paralysed. Then he goes quickly into the back room.*

Yang Sun (*to the audience*) Pregnant . . . ! It's unbelievable. I've been made a fool of. Shui Ta's packed her off somewhere. It's unnatural, it's . . . it's inhumane. I have a son. A small Yang about to enter the world. But the girl's disappeared and I've been left to rot. (*Losing his temper.*) The bastards tried to buy me off with a hat! (*He tramples on it.*) Criminals! Thieves! Kidnappers! And the girl will have no one to protect her.

Sobbing is heard from the back room. He goes still.

Is that someone crying? Who's there? It's stopped. It can't be Shui Ta . . . Who is it? And who's putting the rice out every morning? Is she still here? Is he hiding her? Who else could it be? That would be a gift from the Gods. If she's here, I'll find her, I'll bloody well find her.

Shui Ta *returns from the back room. He goes to the door and looks out into the rain.*

Yang Sun So where is she then?

Shui Ta (*raises his hand and listens*) One moment. It's nine o'clock. You can't hear a thing today. The rain's too strong.

Yang Sun (*with irony*) What're you wanting to hear?

Shui Ta   The mail plane.

Yang Sun   You being funny?

Shui Ta   I was told once you wanted to fly. What happened?

Yang Sun (*cautiously*)   What kind of question's that? You want to buy me off with a pilot's job now? You think I can fly like this? (*Holds up his shaking hands.*) Where's my fiancée? D'you hear me? Where's my fiancée, Shen Te?

Shui Ta   You really want to know?

Yang Sun   Course I do! And I'm telling you now, there'll be no looking the other way if I find out she's been abducted or kidnapped by you.

Pause.

Shui Ta   What would you do?

Yang Sun (*roughly*)   I'd say give me what I want and no more stalling.

Shui Ta   Give you . . .

Yang Sun (*hoarsely*)   The stuff I came for.

Shui Ta   I see. (*Pause.*) I'll never give you any of it.

Yang Sun   Surely your cousin wouldn't deny the father of her child a few pipes and a bench to sleep on? Brother-in-law, my longing for her is overpowering me. I need to do something, I need to hold her in my arms again. Shen Te! Shen Te!

Shui Ta   She's left here. Go and look in the back room.

Yang Sun (*looks at him suspiciously*)   No, not on my own. I'm not in the physical state I used to be. I'll get the police – they're better nourished.

He leaves quickly, making sure not to turn his back on **Shui Ta**.

Shui Ta *watches him, impassively, then goes into the back room and brings out* **Shen Te**'s *belongings: underwear, toiletries, a dress. For a long time he looks at the blue shawl. He rolls everything into a bundle, gets out a suitcase and some men's clothes and packs them in the suitcase.*

Shui Ta   So this is it. After all my effort and so much success I have to leave this profitable business which I built up from that shabby little shop that the Gods thought was sufficient reward for me. One moment of weakness, a stupid moment of indulgence has destroyed everything. I let that idiot open his deceiving mouth instead of handing him in for the theft of three hundred dollars. Toughness, inhumanity are nothing if they're not absolute. That's how the world works.

A noise from outside. He hides the things under the table. A stone is thrown through the window. The voices of a mob outside.

Yang Sun, Wang *and the* **Policeman** *enter.*

Policeman   Mr Shui Ta, due to the excitable mood in the neighbourhood I'm being forced to investigate an allegation against you – that you're holding your cousin, Miss Shen Te, against her will.

Shui Ta   Nonsense.

Policeman   Mr Yang Sun here says he heard sobbing from the room behind your office, sobbing sounds which could only have been made by a woman. With your permission, I'd like to inspect the room.

Shui Ta *opens the door. The* **Policeman** *bows and steps onto the threshold. He looks into the room, then turns round and smiles.*

Policeman   No one there.

Yang Sun   But I heard sobbing . . .

He notices the things under the table.

They weren't there before.

He opens the bundle and pulls out **Shen Te***'s clothing etc.*

Wang   Those are Shen Te's clothes.

He runs to the door and shouts to the mob outside.

Her clothes are here!

Policeman   You said that your cousin had left town, Mr Shui Ta. Tell us where we can find her.

Shui Ta   I don't have her address.

Policeman   Just give me something, anything to shut them up.

Mob   They've found Shen Te's things! The Tobacco King has murdered and hidden the girl!

Policeman   Mr Shui Ta, you'll have to come with me to the police station.

Shui Ta *bows and leaves the house in front of the* **Policeman**.

Wang   A terrible crime has been committed.

Yang Sun (*confused*)   But I heard sobbing . . .

Interlude

Wang's *sleeping place.*

Music. For the last time the **Gods** *appear to* **Wang** *in his sleep.*

The signs of miles of wandering, deep exhaustion and many bad experiences are unmistakable. One God has lost his hat, one has lost a leg in a fox trap and all three are barefoot.

Wang   You're here at last. Oh, Divinities, terrible things are happening in Shen Te's shop. She's disappeared and her cousin's taken control of everything. Now he's been arrested and people are saying he murdered her for the shop. But I don't believe it. She was in a dream I had and she told me that her cousin's holding her captive. You have to return to us and free her.

First God   This is terrible! Our whole journey has been a failure. We found so few good people and they were all living in conditions not fit for human beings. Shen Te was our only hope.

Second God   If she's still good, that is.

Wang   Course she is – but we can't find her anywhere . . . !

First God   Then everything is lost.

Second God   We need courage.

First God   Courage? If she isn't found we'll have to resign. What kind of world did we find? Misery, baseness and ruin everywhere. Even the landscape dying. The beautiful trees have been replaced by pylons and beyond the mountain we saw clouds of black smoke and heard gunfire. And nowhere a good person succeeding.

Third God   Oh, water seller, is this what our commands do? I fear all our moral rules may have to be scrapped. The people have enough to do living their barren lives. Good intentions drive them to the edge, good deeds push them over. (*To the other two* **Gods**.) The world is truly uninhabitable, you must concede that now.

First God (*vehemently*)   No, it's because the people are worthless!

Third God   It's because the world is too cold.

Second God   It's because the people are too weak.

First God   Dignity, my friends, keep your dignity. We must not despair. We found one, didn't we? One who was good and who didn't become evil. If she's missing, then we will not rest until we find her. One is enough – one good soul will be enough.

They disappear swiftly.

Nine

A courtroom.

In groups: **Shu Fu** *and the tobacco merchant* **Mi Tsu***;* **Mrs Shin** *and the* **Agent** *together with the* **Policeman***;* **Wang** *with the family of eight, the* **Carpenter** *and the* **Young Prostitute** *and her* **Mother***.* **Yang Sun** *is by himself.*

Grandfather   Shui Ta's too powerful.

Wang   I got as many witnesses together as I could.

Carpenter   The Tobacco King has the same powerful friends as the Judge.

Sister-in-Law   Mrs Shin was seen last night outside the Judge's house, handing in a huge goose. The fat was dripping through the basket.

Young Prostitute   Poor Shen Te will never be found, will she?

Wang   The Gods are the only ones who could uncover the truth.

Policeman   Silence in court!

The **Gods** *enter, wearing robes, whispering as they walk to take their seats.*

Third God   We'll be found out. They'll see through the forged certificates.

Second God   And they're going to question the Judge's sudden stomach ache.

First God   No, that's real – he ate half a goose.

Mrs Shin (*alarmed*)   We've got three new judges.

Wang   Three very distinguished judges . . .

The **Third God***, who's the last in the row, overhears and smiles at* **Wang***. The* **Gods** *sit. The* **First God** *slams his gavel on the table. The* **Policeman** *fetches* **Shui Ta***, who's received with hisses. He maintains an arrogant attitude.*

Policeman (*quietly, to* **Shui Ta**)   You won't like this. It's not Judge Fu Yi Tchen. But the new ones look very cooperative.

Shui Ta *sees the* **Gods** *and faints.*

Young Prostitute   What's going on? The Tobacco King's fainted.

Sister-in-Law   Soon as he saw the new judges.

Wang   Does he know them? No, he can't know them.

First God   Are you the tobacco merchant Shui Ta?

Shui Ta (*feebly*)   Yes.

First God   You've been accused of having got rid of your own cousin, Miss Shen Te, in order to take over her shop. Do you plead guilty?

Shui Ta   No.

First God (*looks through the files*)   First we'll hear what the local policeman has to say about the reputations of the defendant and his cousin.

Policeman   Shen Te was a girl who did her best to be pleasant to everyone, who lived and let live, as they say. Whereas Mr Shui Ta is a man of strong principles. His cousin's kindness to people forced him on occasion to . . . get tough. However, Mr Shui Ta, unlike the girl, is a respectable citizen who honours the law.

First God   Are there any others here willing to testify on behalf of the defendant?

Shu Fu *and* **Mi Tsu** *step forward.*

Policeman (*whispers to the* **Gods**)   Mr Shu Fu, a highly influential gentleman.

Shu Fu   Mr Shui Ta is considered a very respectable businessman in this town. He is Vice President of the Chamber of Commerce and has been selected as a Justice of the Peace in his neighbourhood.

Wang (*interrupting*)   By you! 'Cause you do business with him!

Policeman (*whispers about* **Wang**)   A dodgy character.

Mi Tsu   As the president of the charitable society I'd like to bring to the attention of the court the fact that Mr Shui Ta provides both employment and food to many inhabitants of Szechuan.

Policeman (*whispers*)   Mrs Mi Tsu, a close friend of Judge Fu Yi Tchen.

First God   Has anyone present anything to say against the defendant?

Wang, *the* **Carpenter** *and the family of eight step forward.*

Policeman   This lot are the scum of the neighbourhood.

First God   Pertaining to the general conduct of Shui Ta, what do you have to say?

All   He ruined us. / He blackmailed me. / He brought misery. / He exploited the helpless. / Lied. / Deceived. / Murdered.

First God   Defendant, what is your response?

Shui Ta   Your Honour, I did nothing except ensure the survival of my cousin. I only ever appeared three times – each time when she was in danger of losing her shop. I never wanted to stay – it was circumstances that forced me to. And I got nothing but grief for it. My cousin was popular, maybe, but I did the dirty work. That's why I'm hated.

Sister-in-Law   Yes, you are. Take our case, Your Honour! (*To* **Shui Ta**.) I won't mention the sacks.

Shui Ta   Why not? Why not?

Sister-in-Law (*to the* **Gods**)   Shen Te gave us shelter – then *he* had us arrested.

Shui Ta   You were stealing cakes!

Sister-in-Law   He doesn't care about cakes, he was after the shop!

Shui Ta   Yes, you hear that? A *shop*, not a dosshouse.

Sister-in-Law   But we had nowhere to stay.

Shui Ta   There were too many of you. The lifeboat was capsizing so I had to set it afloat again. There wasn't a morning when the poorest of the neighbourhood didn't get their rice. My cousin considered the shop a gift of the Gods.

Wang   And you still wanted to sell it!

Shui Ta   Because my cousin wanted to help a pilot to fly. I was helping her raise the money.

Wang   Maybe that's what she wanted, but you were wanting that well-paid job in Beijing. The shop wasn't good enough for you.

Shui Ta   My cousin knew nothing about business.

Mrs Shin   And she was in love with the pilot.

Shui Ta   She shouldn't have the right to love?

Wang   Of course! So, why did you force her to marry a man she didn't love – the barber over there?

Shui Ta   Because the man she did love was no good.

First God   Is he here?

Mrs Shin (*points to* **Yang Sun**)   There. The proverb says birds of a feather flock together. He's what your Angel of the Suburbs got up to in private.

Wang (*angrily*)   She didn't love him because he was like her, it was because he was so downcast. She didn't help him because she was in love with him, she loved him *because* she helped him.

Second God   You're right. To love like that was worthy of her.

Shui Ta   But it was too dangerous. It destroyed her!

First God   Is this pilot accusing you of Shen Te's murder?

Yang Sun   No, false imprisonment! He can't have killed her. I heard her voice just before he was arrested.

First God   Tell us exactly what you heard?

Yang Sun   Sobbing, Your Honour, sobbing.

Third God   And you recognised it as hers?

Yang Sun   I know her voice.

Shu Fu   You made her cry often enough.

Yang Sun   I made her happy too. But then he . . . (*points to* **Shui Ta**) wanted to sell her to you.

Shui Ta (*to* **Yang Sun**)   Because you didn't love her.

Yang Sun   I had no job.

Wang (*to* **Shui Ta**)   You were only after the barber's money.

Shui Ta   But ask what the money was needed for, Your Honour. (*To* **Yang Sun**.) You wanted her to sacrifice everything for you – but the barber offered his houses and his money to help the poor. And if she'd married him, she could've done even more good. But she didn't want to.

Wang   So now it's Shen Te's fault?

Shui Ta   Yes. It usually was.

Mrs Shin   Look at all the good she did. Look at that junkie there who she wanted to help! (*Points to* **Yang Sun**.) And look at him . . . (*Points to the* **Agent**.) Mr Li Gung. Less than a year ago he came into her shop in rags, unemployed and begging for a cigarette. Now he's working as a commercial agent for Mr Shui Ta.

Agent (*standing up*)   It's true. It was Mr Shui Ta helped me get where I am today.

Prostitute's Mother (*to her daughter*)   That's him, isn't it?

The daughter nods.

He's a heroin dealer. He works for Mr Shui Ta. We have proof.

Wang   It's typical of the way you 'help' people, Mr Shui Ta. Shen Te had to be got rid of so you could build up your heroin empire. Tell the court the truth.

Shui Ta   It's for the child.

Wife   What child?

Carpenter   What about *our* kids, Tobacco King? Slaving in your sweat shops!

Shui Ta *is silent. The* **Grandfather** *steps forward at a sign from* **Wang**.

Grandfather (*dignified*)   The work is unhealthy. The boy coughs constantly.

Wang   That shut you up. The Gods gave Shen Te that shop to be a source of good in the world. But every time she tried, you were there to block her.

Shui Ta (*enraged*)   Because otherwise the source would have dried up, you fool!

Mrs Shin   He's right, Your Honour.

Wang   What use is a source if the water kills you?

Shui Ta   Good deeds bring ruin.

Wang   So bad deeds mean a good life, is that right? What did you do with her, you evil bastard?

Shui Ta   I was her only friend.

All   Where is she?

Shui Ta   Gone away!

Wang   Where?

Shui Ta   I won't tell you.

All   But why did she have to go?

Shui Ta (*shouts*)   Because all of you would've torn her to pieces!

A sudden silence. **Shui Ta** *collapses into his chair.*

I can't go on any more. I'll explain everything. If the judges clear the courtroom, I'll make a confession.

All   He's confessing. / He's been found guilty.

First God (*slams his gavel*)   Clear the courtroom.

The **Policeman** *clears the courtroom.*

Mrs Shin (*as she goes*)   They're in for a surprise.

Shui Ta   Have they gone? All of them? I can't be silent any more. I recognise you, Divinities.

Second God   What have you done with our good soul of Szechuan?

Shui Ta   I must tell the truth. I'm her.

He takes his mask off and pulls off his clothes. **Shen Te** *stands before them.*

Second God   Shen Te!

Shen Te
Yes, it's me. Shui Ta and Shen Te.

The instruction you gave me
To live and be good
Has ripped me apart like a lightning bolt.
I couldn't do it,
It was too hard – to be good to others
And to myself at the same time.
Your world is so tough.
So much misery, so much despair.

Hold out your hand to help
And it will be torn off.
Help the people who are lost
And you become lost yourself.
Who couldn't resist being bad
If they know they'll die hungry?
Where was I to find the strength that was needed?
Only from myself! But I wasn't strong enough.
The weight of good intentions crushed me.

When I did wrong I walked around proudly,
My stomach full of fine food.
Something is wrong with your world.
Why is wickedness rewarded?
Why are the good punished so harshly?
Oh, I was so tempted to think only of myself.
I had a secret knowledge inside me,
Because my mother used to wash me in the gutter
All my senses were sharp as steel.

But pity hurt me so acutely
That I became furious at the sight of misery.
Then I felt myself changing,
My lips becoming hard and thin
And kind words tasted bitter in my mouth.
And yet I wanted to be an Angel of the Suburbs.
One happy face and I was walking on air.

Condemn me – all I did was help my neighbours
and love the man I loved
and try to save my little son from poverty.
For your grand plan, O Gods,
I was human – too human and too small.

First God (*with all the signs of outrage*)   Enough. We were so happy to find you again – what are we to think now?

Shen Te   I'm a bad person hated by everyone in Szechuan.

First God   You're the good soul of Szechuan loved by everyone.

Shen Te   The bad one too!

First God   It was a misunderstanding! A few unfortunate events . . . You were perhaps a bit overenthusiastic.

Second God   But how will she go on living?

First God   She is a strong person – and tough. She can do it.

Second God   Didn't you hear what she said?

First God (*vehemently*)   So much confusion. It's unbelievable. Do we have to admit our commands are fatal? Should we scrap them? No. Is the world to be changed? How? By whom? No, everything is in order. (*Slams his gavel down.*) And now . . .

At a sign from him, music is heard. A rosy glow is seen.

> Let us return.
> We've found this little world fascinating.
> Its joys and suffering
> Have delighted and pained us.
> And beyond the stars and planets, Shen Te,
> We will think of you often.
> Shen Te, the good person,
> Who makes our spirit manifest down here on earth.
> Carrier of a small burning light in the cold darkness.
> Farewell, goodbye.

At a sign from him the ceiling opens. A pink cloud descends. The **Gods** *get on it and are slowly lifted upwards.*

Shen Te   Don't go! Don't leave! Don't leave me! How am I going to look the water seller in the face? What about the barber who I'll never love? And what do I do about Yang Sun? And I'm pregnant and I'm having the child soon and he'll have to eat. I can't stay here!

She looks in panic towards the door, through which are the neighbours and others.

First God   You can do it. Just be good and everything will be fine.

Everyone enters. They stare amazed to see the **Gods** *floating upwards on their pink cloud.*

Wang   Show your respect! The Gods have appeared among us. Three of the most eminent Gods came to Szechuan to look for a good person and they found one . . .

First God   And there she is.

All   Shen Te!

First God   Not dead, only in hiding. She will remain among you, the good soul of Szechuan.

Shen Te   But I need my cousin!

First God   No, you don't.

Shen Te   Please. Just once a week.

First God   Once a month then, no more.

Shen Te   Oh, don't leave, Divinities! I haven't told you everything yet. I need you so badly.

The **Gods** *sing the 'Trio of the Vanishing Gods on a Cloud'.*

Gods
　　The time has come, we must depart
　　Now is the hour to take our leave
　　Further studied and examined
　　Our virtuous find may disappear

　　Human bodies cast dark shadows
　　And obscure the golden light
　　Therefore now you must allow us
　　Home to our eternal life.

Shen Te   Help me!

Gods
　　Let us now the search is over
　　Leave quickly while we can
　　All on earth raise your voices
　　Praise the good soul of Szechuan.

While **Shen Te** *desperately stretches to reach them, they disappear upwards, smiling and waving.*

Methuen Drama Student Editions

Methuen Drama Modern Plays

include work by

Edward Albee
Jean Anouilh
John Arden
Margaretta D'Arcy
Peter Barnes
Sebastian Barry
Brendan Behan
Dermot Bolger
Edward Bond
Bertolt Brecht
Howard Brenton
Anthony Burgess
Simon Burke
Jim Cartwright
Caryl Churchill
Noël Coward
Lucinda Coxon
Sarah Daniels
Nick Darke
Nick Dear
Shelagh Delaney
David Edgar
David Eldridge
Dario Fo
Michael Frayn
John Godber
Paul Godfrey
David Greig
John Guare
Peter Handke
David Harrower
Jonathan Harvey
Iain Heggie
Declan Hughes
Terry Johnson
Sarah Kane
Charlotte Keatley
Barrie Keeffe
Howard Korder

Robert Lepage
Doug Lucie
Martin McDonagh
John McGrath
Terrence McNally
David Mamet
Patrick Marber
Arthur Miller
Mtwa, Ngema & Simon
Tom Murphy
Phyllis Nagy
Peter Nichols
Sean O'Brien
Joseph O'Connor
Joe Orton
Louise Page
Joe Penhall
Luigi Pirandello
Stephen Poliakoff
Franca Rame
Mark Ravenhill
Philip Ridley
Reginald Rose
Willy Russell
Jean-Paul Sartre
Sam Shepard
Wole Soyinka
Simon Stephens
Shelagh Stephenson
Peter Straughan
C. P. Taylor
Theatre de Complicite
Theatre Workshop
Sue Townsend
Judy Upton
Timberlake Wertenbaker
Roy Williams
Snoo Wilson
Victoria Wood

Methuen Drama Contemporary Dramatists

include

CPSIA information can be obtained at www.ICGtesting.com
Printed in the USA
LVOW06s2032110815

449712LV00014B/285/P